DNA

Q & A

Real questions,
From real people
About genetic genealogy

Other Books by Devon Noel Lee

21st Century Family Historian

Power Scrapbooking

Family History Scrapbooking Simplified

From Metal to Rhinestones: A Quest for the Crown

Other Books by Andrew Lee

How to Fail English with Style

Other Books by Andrew Lee & Devon Noel Lee

A Recipe for Writing Family History

reimagine Family History

DNA
Q & A

Real questions,
From real people
About genetic genealogy

Andrew Lee &
Devon Noel Lee

DNA Q&A: Real Questions From Real People About Genetic Genealogy

Published by FHF Group LLC

Table of Contents

Introduction

The year 2017 may go down as '**The Year of DNA**' in genealogy circles. The year started with a few million samples in the major databases, but the database sizes of AncestryDNA, 23andMe, Family Tree DNA, and MyHeritage DNA grew tremendously. The likely trigger for the growth was a competitive risk taken in February. One company offered their DNA kits at the RootsTech genealogy conference for an unprecedented low price of $49.

By December, every genetic testing company had discounted the kit price to $49-59 at least once. Over the weekend of Black Friday, genetic testing companies sold more than 3 million DNA test kits. 3 million amounts to more kits sold in one weekend than the total number of test kits purchased in the three years before 2017. As 2018 began, the principal databases collectively had nearly 15 million samples.

DNA was the most popular genealogy topic of 2016 and 2017, and that trend looks to continue for the foreseeable future. Every major conference has standing room only DNA workshops. Several conventions are dedicated solely to genetic genealogy. 2018 schedules for libraries, genealogical societies, and conferences have an incredible increase in the number of genetic genealogy sessions.

One thing I have found from teaching people about genetic genealogy is that the questions never end. Although some issues are repetitive, each class I teach always brings up a query that I had not thought about before. Some of this may be from participants misunderstanding the science behind DNA. Other repetitive questions stem from new people joining this genetic community and learning 'common' knowledge for the first time. Since the Human Genome Project was completed in 2003 (two years ahead of schedule), the field of genetics, and by extension genetic genealogy, has progressed rapidly. Who knew biology could attract so much interest?

Commercial genetic testing is here to stay and with it will be all of the inquiries people have. While there are several books about genetic genealogy methodology, this book focuses on real questions from real people and my answers. The questions come from the Family History Fanatics YouTube channel, online workshops, and live presentations I have led.

These are real questions, from real people brave enough to ask what they do not understand. I have reworded them to be more clear and concise or to protect the privacy of the inquisitive minds. Not every question and answer will pertain to your situation, but you can probably find your answer from the many similar queries. If you are beginning your genetic genealogy journey, then perhaps these conversations will help you along the way.

I did not extensively research every response in this book. The Q&As were conversations with replies answered off the cuff based on my knowledge of DNA. It was interesting as I compiled all of the questions and answers for this book how many times I misspoke or said something that was utterly false. We all do that from time to time. I have been able to correct most of my mistakes but that in no way implies that the answers in this book are flawless.

I should not be your sole source for DNA information. In fact, I have not included a list of references for that reason. Since almost all of these answers were off the top of my head, use them as a starting point in your learning. The International Society of Genetic Genealogy website and Wikipedia are great resources to find more information about specific genetic genealogy topics.

If you do not find your question in this book, then leave a comment on our YouTube channel or send me an email at info@familyhistoryfanatics.com. I just might make a video about it in the future.

Basic Science

Is the genetic test administered at a hospital the same as the DNA tests offered by 23andMe, AncestryDNA, and Family Tree DNA?

Hospital and medical DNA tests are not going to be transferable to the genealogical companies. Usually, if you are testing for a medical reason (like the risk of breast cancer), the test searches for variants that are indicative of that condition. Knowing whether you have the three genetic mutations that significantly increase your risk of having breast cancer is beneficial for your medical health. However, knowing those genetic markers tells you nothing genealogically, cannot be used to match with other individuals, and will not reveal ethnicity percentages. There is just not enough information.

To take a genealogical DNA test, visit the website of one of the four companies listed in your question. Order a kit. Create your sample by using the cheek swab or spitting in a test tube. Ship it to the company. Review your results on their website in a few weeks.

Will DNA testing save me from doing genealogical research?

No.

There are some cool techniques you can use to build a tree with DNA information on people you do not know, but DNA definitely will not create a tree for you. When you combine DNA results with genealogical research, you can map out your tree in places that may have been difficult before.

Think of DNA as a genealogical record. It might tell you considerable information, but no single document is going to have the information you need to build a family tree.

Why are these companies pushing the availability and simplicity of these kits?

DNA is a record of relationships. DNA tests create a valuable genealogical record because there is no limit to the number of family members that one DNA sample can identify. It is limited only by the number of people that have tested.

Since genealogy companies are interested in furthering people's hobby of research, it makes perfect sense that they would want to make this record easily available to the greatest number of people.

TEST ACCURACY

Are genetic ancestry tests unreliable? After all, they are still in the early stages.

The genetic test itself does a reading of 500,000 to 1,000,000 SNPs. SNPs, pronounced 'snips,' are DNA locations where the genetic differences are known to occur. If you compare the raw data between companies (the SNP readings), the test results are very accurate. For instance, when comparing my 23andMe and my AncestryDNA test results, the companies reported less than 50 locations in the 300,000 common SNPs differently.

Consumer testing companies use that raw data for three different interpretations:

1. Genetic matching - looking at identical DNA sequences between individuals. Genetic matching is reasonably accurate because there is not much manipulation or analysis of the raw data. Some matches are invalid genetic results, usually in the segments of 5 cM and smaller. Some false matches resolve themselves with techniques like phasing and triangulation.

2. Medical or Trait information - examining the raw genetic data and comparing it to previously conducted research studies. The test results are reasonably accurate with a couple of caveats.

   First, a single SNP or gene variation does not define many traits. Traits like hair, eye, and skin color are all related and involve the interaction of dozens of genes, each of which has SNPs to differentiate their respective alleles.
   Second, for many medical conditions, genetics is not the only determining factor. Environmental factors may also play a role. Using these results for any decision making should be done with the advice and review of competent medical professionals.

3. Ethnicity/Heritage/Admixture - compares genetic data to a reference population, and attempts to

match up segments with those in the reference sets. Each company has their own algorithms and reference sets. It is no surprise that the results vary from each business, even when analyzing the same raw data. Sometimes the variance is minor, and sometimes it is significant.

While the marketing departments of testing companies may claim accuracy, the data needed to validate their precision is just not available. The sizes of the reference populations are sufficient for reliable results on a continental level, but not on a country level or smaller geopolitical region.

All those tests are pseudo-scientific chutzpah. Wait 20 years and take a serious test.

That is a little harsh. The scientific study of relationships using DNA is pretty spot-on. What is lacking is a large enough reference population to apply the ethnicity algorithms to and have a high level of confidence beyond the continental level. I agree that in 20 years the results will be much better than today. However, part of the reason those results will be better is because of the data that is gathered from those testing today.

Have you done a double-blind test of any genetic testing company (testing the same DNA with different names with a time gap between submissions)? Wouldn't the results be different?

I would not expect the ethnicity results from the same company to be vastly different. After all, the companies are not shooting in the dark. There is an algorithm behind the numbers; however, the reference populations are not always accurate. The reference sets establish assumptions with which companies model their results.

Since 23andMe has changed the chip they use from when I tested, I would expect different ethnicity results, though not drastically changed. 23andMe is analyzing a different set of SNPs with the new chip, and there is only about 20% overlap between the V3 chip and the current V5 chip. I do notice a disparity in my 23andMe and AncestryDNA results. However, this is only on the smaller than continental level. Both tell me I am predominantly (99%) European.

CELLULAR SCIENCE

What are "segments"?

Each person has a set of chromosomes from their mother and another from their father. Before a chromosome is passed on to you, it reshuffles places. This reshuffling mixes the DNA from your father's parents or your mother's parents. Thus the chromosome you receive from dad is recombined DNA from grandma and grandpa. Across your 23 chromosomes pairs, Dad's chromosome pairs with a similarly recombined chromosome from Mom.

In the end, your DNA is unique from what your mother, father, and grandparents had. However, you have pieces of DNA that you share with each of your parents and grandparents. Those genetic pieces are called segments.

Whenever you genetically match with other relatives, companies find similar segments of DNA between each of you which indicate a shared relation. In short, a segment is a piece of DNA that two or more people inherited from a common ancestor.

Why do my results only show 23 chromosomes when there are actually 46 combined into pairs?

Most companies display 46 individual chromosomes as 23 pairs because the data has not been phased, or divided between mother and father contributions. Without phasing, you just have a list of SNP readings. You can not tell which SNP reading (i.e., AT AT AT AT AT) belongs on the father's chromosome or the mother's. AAAAA and TTTTT could be correct, but so could AAATT and TTTAA or ATATA and TATAT.

The testing websites that show unphased data as two chromosomes (one pair) are guessing as to how to divide up the SNP readings. Depending on how closely related the parents are, this may be a reasonable approximation or a grossly inaccurate.

How many total centimorgans (cMs) should I share with my grandfather?

Based on Blaine Bettinger's Shared cM project you share between 1156 and 2311 cM with each grandparent. I share 1754 cM with my paternal grandfather, which is smack dab in the middle of the range expected.

I have read that when you take DNA tests at different ent companies, they do not scan your whole DNA. They only look at some random parts of it and process our results from that. Is that accurate?

You are mostly correct. The human genome has 3 billion base pairs, of which about 99.9% are the same for every human. The remaining 3 million base pairs are unique between individuals. As such, companies do not scan your whole DNA because 99.9% of the scan would be wasted effort.

The differing 3 million base pairs are spread across several million locations with possible unique sites (also called SNPs). Each of the testing companies uses a microarray chip that looks at 500,000-750,000 of these SNPs. In short, SNPs are not selected and processed at random.

If you and your brother test at AncestryDNA, the company evaluates the same 500,000 unique SNPs for both of you. The overlap between the businesses is on the order of 150,000 - 450,000 SNPs depending on when and where you took your test.

When would I want to take a Y-DNA test?

Unless you have a specific genealogy question on your patrilineal line, Y-DNA testing (no matter the type) is going to provide you trivial information.

From a tree building standpoint, Y-DNA is also of limited use. While it can certainly look back far further than the 5-7 generations you receive with autosomal testing, beyond about 20 generations, there is no credible paper trail for practically every line. Beyond 40 generations, there is no reliable paper trail for any family tree to corroborate with your Y-DNA results.

If on the other hand, you want to connect yourself to some distant ancestor, (like the Stuart clan), then Y-DNA testing (or in some rare cases mitochondrial DNA testing) is the only way.

If Y-DNA is passed from father to son, and my father is dead, and I am a female, then how do I find out my dad's heritage? How do I even know if my dad was my dad?

The Y-DNA test is only useful for a specific genealogy question on your patrilineal line.

If your mom is still living, have her autosomal DNA tested. Then review your results for people to which you match, but your mom does not. These matches will be your father's heritage, including but not limited to the Y-DNA relations.

You can also have any relative from your father's line tested, again with the autosomal DNA test. If you match these results, then you know he is likely your father.

What is X-DNA and what does it reveal?

X-DNA is usually lumped in with the autosomal DNA. It is the bastard stepchild of the DNA world. X-DNA comes from the sex chromosome. Males inherit one X-chromosome and females inherit two. Inheritance is not clear-cut in the X-DNA because at the 7th generation a male could have potentially 21 ancestors who provided his X chromosome and females have 34. With Y-DNA, only one man in each generation could have provided the Y chromosome. The same principles hold true with mtDNA, but only for women.

X-DNA is useful for eliminating branches of your family tree from which distant cousins are related. Because of its inheritance pattern, an X-DNA match, without a corresponding autosomal connection, is probably outside of a genealogically significant timescale.

Family Tree DNA uses a STR test for Y-DNA and 23andMe uses a SNP test. Both provide you your paternal haplogroup. How is that possible?

The SNPs test determines the actual haplogroup assignment. The STR Y-DNA tests are used to predict the haplogroup.

While comparing known haplogroups to their STR predictions, the STR results can fairly reliably match individuals to their haplogroups.

My daughter has the mtDNA haplotype "R" and mine is "H16". What is your opinion on how this error could happen?

The first possible reason is that the H haplogroup descends from the R haplogroup. So, it is not an error but a result of inheritance. If one of you had some "non-matching" SNPs that distinguish R from H16, then you would be assigned different haplogroups.

The second possibility is that 23andMe changed their testing chip in August 2017. As such, the different mtDNA SNPs that 23andMe tests for produced a slightly different haplogroup for the two of you (although within the same branch of the haplogroup tree).

Without doing a full mitochondrial DNA test from Family Tree DNA, you would not be able to tell which one it is (although I suspect it is the H16 since that is a daughter haplogroup of R).

Do haplogroups come from specific countries?

Haplogroups can originate anywhere. While there may be a few isolated groups in particular countries, the vast majority of the haplogroups span large swaths of the globe.

The entire autosomal genome is the basis for the ethnicity/admixture results. The haplogroup is determined using only the Y chromosome or the Mitochondrial DNA.

I have heard testing companies take samples from old cemeteries. Wouldn't that lead to inaccurate matches and ethnicities? How would we know if the corpses belonged to the name listed on the gravestone?

No genetic genealogy testing companies use data from cemeteries. Perhaps some archaeological information but not any modern cemeteries. While grave robbing was a semi-profitable venture back in the 18th and 19th century, that is not the case today.

EVOLUTIONARY DNA

Is it true that scientists have discovered an Adam and Eve? Not the Garden of Eden Biblical couple, but the biological Adam found by tracing the Y Chromosome and biological Eve by tracing the Mitochondrial DNA over hundreds of thousands of years? And, is it also true that Y-DNA Adam and Mt-DNA Eve were not inhabiting the earth at the same time?

Y-DNA Adam and Mitochondrial Eve were the male and female that are responsible for our Y chromosome and our mitochondrial DNA respectively. They were not the first humans (both had mothers and fathers) but rather the most recent common paternal and maternal ancestor of everyone living today.

Y-DNA Adam and Mitochondrial Eve were also not the only humans of their time/generation that contributed to the DNA of everyone alive today. Most if not all of your autosomal DNA came from the other humans who lived at the same time-period as them.

Finally, Y-DNA Adam and Mitochondrial Eve did not live at the same time. Y-DNA Adam has been estimated to have lived about 250,000 years ago while Mitochondrial Eve was around 125,000 years ago. There are some similarities with the biblical story where they take their names, but enough differences that people often become confused.

I took a DNA test, and I am supposed to have Neanderthal and Denisovan DNA, but they do not show up in my results. Do I not have these types of DNA?

Did you test with 23andMe? 23andMe reports the Neanderthal variants. I do not think any of the other genealogy companies do. It is a separate report from the ethnicity report.

For point of reference, unless all of your ancestors are from Africa, you have Neanderthal DNA. Denisovan DNA is not as widespread as Neanderthal DNA.

How could we possibly be 99.9% the same geneti-cally, if some people have considerable Nean-derthal and Denisovan DNA while others have none?

First, let's understand the biological similarities of modern and ancient humans. Modern humans (homo sapien sapiens) are different from Neanderthals (homo sapien neanderthal) or Denisovan (homo sapien deniso-van). Without having seen the statistics, I would guess that we are 99.0 - 99.5% the same as both of these archaic humans.

That was the simple part of the explanation. The rest of the question can be a little confusing to answer.

Compare me (roughly 2.7% Neanderthal the way 23andMe used to report it) and someone from Nigeria (0% Neanderthal). Initially, you would think that the most we could be the same is 97.3% because of the Neanderthal DNA. However, the percentages are look-ing at different things. The 99.9% is looking at the entire string of letters individually, while the 2.7% is looking at genes or large chunks of DNA collectively.

To simplify it, 2.7% of my genes may have come from Neanderthals, but (using 99% similarity between Neanderthals and modern humans) the majority of the letters in those genes are identical between humans and Neanderthals. You could have a gene that is 1000 letters long, and the Neanderthal variant is ten letters different from the human variant $(1-(10/1000)=99\%)$. Since this only affects, 2.7% of my genes, that 1% difference contributes 0.027% to the overall variance which is well within the 0.1% difference that any two humans have.

While watching the PBS show with Professor Gates, I noticed that he said that their DNA biology search traces back five hundred years. So how many years does the AncestryDNA test trace back in time?

Those years are based on haplogroups which only cover your paternal line (father's father's father...) or maternal line (mother's mother's mother...).

AncestryDNA does not give you haplogroups, so it will not help you stretch back that far in time. Their autosomal test is useful for matching with cousins out to about six generations which amounts to approximately 200 years.

DNA has a half-life of approximately 521 years. Can you process reference DNA samples from a mummy that is 1 million years old?

Usually, DNA is considered gone in ten half-lives. I have heard of scientists recovering DNA from mummies that are nearly 5,000 years old, but not from anything that is close to 1 million years old. Even at 5,000 years, the DNA is fragmented and not representative of a complete genome. So, scientists can not process reference DNA from that time frame.

MEDICAL ISSUES

Have you any knowledge of DNA damage that would have adverse effects on tracing my origins with DNA? I had chemotherapy and radiation treatments a few years ago. Many of the side effects lingered until the last couple of years. I have read that permanent damage can occur to our DNA.

Yes, chemotherapy and radiation can damage DNA. In fact, that is the mechanism that makes them effective against cancer cells. However, these types of treatments are usually localized, targeted to a specific tissue or cancerous growth. Radiation is applied with pinpoint accuracy, and chemotherapy treatments are formulated based on the particular cancer location to minimize side effects to the rest of the body.

Nonetheless, cells have a very powerful mechanism for repairing themselves (including their DNA). All of the genealogical tests use saliva, which will contain some cells from your cheeks or tongue. Unless you had chemotherapy or radiation for throat cancer or mouth cancer within the last week or so, then DNA test results after the treatment would match results from before. I do not know for sure, but I suspect that even immediately after chemotherapy or radiation, that the DNA test would show up the same. Based on your treatment history, taking a DNA test several years later would be as accurate as taking one before your chemotherapy and radiation treatments.

Do bone marrow transplants or organ transplants change your DNA?

Transplants change the DNA for that organ, or in the case of bone marrow transplants, the blood. Blood transfusions also introduce a different DNA makeup into your bloodstream. If you took a blood-based DNA test, then it would have a different DNA makeup that would probably look confusing. The results would resemble two people (you and the person you received the transplant or blood from). None of the consumer genealogical companies use a blood-based test.

Consumer genealogical tests use a saliva sample which collects cells within your mouth. One of the things they ask you to do is not eat or drink for 30 minutes beforehand. The idea behind this is that your natural saliva production will flush out any food bits from a meal so that you are not testing the hamburger you ate!

WHO SHOULD TEST

I have a 93-year-old great-aunt, but I am reluctant to ask her to take a test as I doubt I could explain it to her. Is it moral or ethical to request a DNA sample from someone who may not understand it?

If they do not understand it, don't request it. That is the call you will have to make in your family.

How you approach the topic can help people understand. If you break it down in simple terms, most people who do not have a mental deficiency should be able to understand it as a genealogical record. Talk about genealogy and finding extended relatives through the test. Relate DNA to a record of your family members like a birth certificate documents your birth.

I had my 80-year-old grandparents tested. All they cared about was that it might help solve genealogy mysteries. My grandma even insisted on paying for it! A year later my grandpa died. Three months after that we discovered who his grandfather was with the DNA he had provided.

Your advice strongly emphasizes testing the oldest generation first. Is this ALWAYS best? Do different rules apply to Y-DNA, mtDNA, and other kinds of DNA tests?

Test oldest first is always best unless you have a specific problem you are trying to solve and have identified others who could potentially solve that problem. Reasons, why oldest is best, are as follows:

1. When they die, their DNA is gone.

2. They have all of the DNA that their descendants have and reach further back on the genetic family tree than younger individuals.

3. The more generations that test, rather than the more individuals within a generation, increases

the length of matching segments between each generation. Longer sequences of matching DNA increase the chances of finding additional relatives.

4. Since Y-DNA and Mitochondrial DNA are passed down without going through recombination, there is no benefit between testing older people or younger people with these tests. There is still the remote possibility a mutation occurred between your grandmother and you. In which case, you would want your grandmother tested to have a better chance of matching with distant relatives.

After collecting samples from every parent and grandparent, testing children and grandchildren yield no additional genealogical information. However, the results do provide an anchor for triangulation. It also confirms that you really are your father's child (sometimes you aren't!).

My paternal grandparents are dead. Whom should I test?

Test your father and his siblings. Each relative will have a unique part of DNA from your grandparents. If your grandparents had siblings that are still living test them as well. The birth order of the siblings does not matter for DNA testing, but if someone is in poor health, make them a priority. Once they are dead, you are not going to obtain their DNA.

Is it worth taking a DNA test if I am adopted? I want to learn from where I come, but I am uncertain about the value of the tests given the lack of accuracy in the ethnicity results.

Yes! The ethnicity results are excellent clues. From a continental and regional level, the results are fairly accurate. However, the value for adoptees is the ability to match DNA with others that may connect you with your biological.

If you have limited funds, test with AncestryDNA ($79-$99 USD), then transfer the results to Family Tree DNA (free-$19), MyHeritage DNA (free), and Gedmatch (also free). Then purchase a Promethease.com report for health information ($5-$10). When you have another $99, then test with 23andMe. That will put you in all of the databases to match with others and be able to use all of their tools. The total price is $227. Don't spend it all at once. If you wait patiently, over a year you can catch sales on AncestryDNA and 23andMe and have the total amount down to $157.

What is the advantage of testing myself, a female, if my brother took the Y-DNA test?

You will benefit from having your DNA tested, but not from a Y-DNA perspective. The Y-DNA is only one of the 46 chromosomes. You share about 50% of your DNA with your brother, but you both you and your brother have unique combinations of your parental chromosomes.

If your brother did an autosomal test (Family Finder, 23andMe, AncestryDNA, MyHeritage DNA), then your results will have some overlap with his, but will also have some differences. In essence, by having both of you test, you are preserving a more significant portion of your parents' DNA to match with potential distant cousins.

I am thinking that testing my brother will capture the Y-DNA (which I do not have as I am female) and my mother to capture her mt-DNA. However, I am considering testing my mother's sister who is still alive. Should I buy kits for all of us or only my mother and brother to generate the maximum genetic information?

If you want to maximize information, then test everyone. The reason is all types of DNA is useful for genetic purposes.

Testing your mother will capture her autosomal DNA (chromosomes 1-22). You have some of this, and your brother has some of this. However, the two of you do not have all of what your mother has.

1. Testing you and your three relatives will allow you to do DNA triangulation. Triangulation will help to separate the false from the actual matches.

2. Testing you and your brother will reveal most of the autosomal DNA of your father (which I am assuming you cannot directly test since you did not mention him). Between the two of you, you will have about 75% of the autosomal DNA from your father. You also carry an X-chromosome from your father (which is the least useful, but still something).

3. As you recognized, testing your brother will get the Y-DNA from your father.

4. Testing your mother and her sister will capture about 75% of the autosomal DNA of your maternal grandparents. (Also useful for triangulation.)

5. Testing all of the people you mentioned will preserve the Mitochondrial DNA, which should be identical so if you are doing a specific Mitochondrial DNA test (through Family Tree DNA) you only need to do one person.

I have the original and translated copies of my father's family hand baptismal records from circa 1500's A.D. Would it be beneficial to do a DNA test to glean more in-depth information?

I have the original and translated copies of my father's family hand baptismal records from circa 1500's A.D. Would it be beneficial to do a DNA test to glean more in-depth information? Genetic genealogy will only reveal information concerning the last 5-7 generations of ancestors. What it can do is help to confirm the paper records you have, and possibly identify any non-paternity events (i.e., where the reported father is not the biological father).

Additionally, you become the foundation to which those from your heritage, especially those lacking a solid paper trail, can connect.

We were thinking of testing our son who is ten years old. What do you advise?

If your parents or grandparents are still alive, I would strongly recommend you test them first (even before yourself). Once they are dead, their DNA is gone. However, I understand wanting to do it for yourself and your children, after all, I tested myself first.

From a genealogical standpoint, testing your son will provide an anchor for finding triangulation groups between you and your husband, but it will not yield any more matches than what is already in your and your husband's result list.

My husband wants to know if he and his brother have the same father...or not. Should he collect samples from himself and his brother and do the Y-DNA test?

I would just take the autosomal test. If your husband and his brother have the same father (and mother), they should show up as brothers. Technically speaking they will have about 50% shared DNA with 25% fully-shared chromosome segments. If they have different fathers, then they will show up as half-brothers or uncle-nephew because they will have 25% shared DNA with no fully-shared chromosome segments.

Y-DNA would not be definitive because if two brothers fathered them, then they would still have the same Y-DNA. If they were half-brothers (same mother but brothers as the fathers), then the autosomal test will reveal about 12% of fully matched segments, and about 37% shared DNA.

In short, the autosomal DNA test would better identify if the brothers have the same father.

If I know my mitochondrial DNA via my mum's National Geographic test results, is it worth paying extra for the full mtDNA sequence?

Not unless you have already done the autosomal testing at all of the major companies (23andMe, Family Tree DNA, AncestryDNA, and MyHeritage DNA). Full sequence mtDNA will tell you very little that you don't already know. Doing the autosomal tests with all of the companies will allow you to match with potentially hundreds of distant cousins that mtDNA does not reveal.

Is there any sense to test our children if my spouse and I have taken a DNA test? Won't they have the same results?

From an ethnicity standpoint, they will each have a slightly different mix of the two of you (but not in the 50% proportional way). The ethnicity test is more a novelty than a necessity.

From a matching standpoint, everyone they match will also match you and your husband (except for false matches).

From a triangulation standpoint (which would be the most important for identifying valid genealogical cousins), they would be invaluable. You will be able to eliminate some of the false matches that AncestryDNA may be presenting to you. However, you would need to use Gedmatch.com to do the triangulation, and all of Ancestry's database is not on Gedmatch.

From a medical standpoint, if you ever plan on using Promethease to review genetic health and medical information, then having their DNA test will be necessary since they only receive 50% from each of you.

So it depends on what you want to learn from the DNA test results.

I do not have any living grandparents, but I could perhaps test their brothers or sisters. Is there any benefit to doing this and, if so, what companies should I use?

Yes! Test them as soon as possible. They will share a significant amount of DNA with your grandparents so while you cannot access your grandparents' DNA, their siblings are the next best thing.

Gedmatch has a tool (Lazarus) that you can use to recreate a person's DNA profile using relatives. The more family members' DNA in the database and the closer related they are to that person, the better the DNA profile will be. So between your grand aunts, grand uncles, parents, aunts, uncles, and cousins, you should be able to create a decent Lazarus kit.

Granted, testing everyone will take some money and time. If you have older relatives, then test them as soon as possible. When they die, you cannot retrieve their DNA.

Any of the major companies will work (Family Tree DNA, AncestryDNA, 23andMe, or MyHeritage DNA). You will need to transfer the raw data files to Gedmatch to create the Lazarus kit of your grandparents.

Testing Companies

I am trying to find a DNA company that uses both a surname and family tree match database. Which one should I choose?

All of them have some capability for surname and or tree matching. The problem I see is only about 10%-30% of people who have tested have put up a tree, linked their DNA to a tree, or listed likely surnames.

Do I receive my test results in the mail?

You receive your results through the internet. You can access them from any computer. For Ancestry and MyHeritage you may need a subscription, but you can always do a one-month subscription, see your results, print them out, download the raw file and not renew the following month. You will not have access to their tools without a subscription.

How do you know what chip is currently being used and which one I was tested on?

You have to dig into the websites to find it. Roberta Estes compiles a list and keeps it up to date on her blog DNA-explained.com. Here are some general guidelines:

Company	Chip Version	Date Started
23andMe	V2	Before Dec. 2010
	V3	Dec. 2010
	V4	Nov. 2013
	V5	Aug. 2017
AncestryDNA	V1	Before May 2016
	V2	May 2016
Family Tree DNA	Same chip	
MyHeritage DNA	Same chip	
Genographic Project	V1	Before Nov. 2016
	V2	Nov. 2016

How fast is DNA research evolving and reducing the cost of the genetic tests? Would it be possible to spend 50 euros to purchase ALL possible results available?

Definitely. 23andMe used to be subscription-based, but they have changed their financial model. AncestryDNA consistently has had sales of $69 and $79. In 2017, every company offered discounts as low as $49. My best guess is that in ten years you might be able to pick them all up for 50 Euros.

If I wait five years, will the price drop and the accuracy increase?

Probably, but if you buy now, you can enjoy five years of match opportunities. If you die within five years and have tested, then hopefully your relatives can still access your account and benefit from the DNA record. If you have not tested, your family members miss out on your DNA, and its ability to unlock the past.

Accuracy improves as each company updates their algorithms when they receive more data. What they report you are today, is not going to be the same thing they say you are in 5 years. Probably close but still not the same.

Why don't all these companies just share their databases?

Companies do not share because their databases are worth money! 23andMe primarily USES their database for medical research. The genealogical competent of the company is a side venture. AncestryDNA, from what I understand, sells ACCESS to their database to researchers. Family Tree DNA is strictly a genealogical company.

Each company optimizes their tools for their database and business goals. Maintaining separate databases is an economics issue. Same reason Coke and Pepsi do not share their formulas with each other.

However, you can compare your test results between the other companies for free by going to GEDmatch.com.

ANCESTRYDNA

What is the accuracy AncestryDNA's test results? What if someone links me as their son or daughter

based on the Ancestry results? Are the results reliable and accurate?

Ethnicity accuracy is iffy. Numerous variables combine to calculate ethnicity, many of which are not very reliable.

Reported relationships between close relatives (parents, siblings, grandparents, aunts, uncles, and cousins through 2nd cousins) are about as accurate as can be, mainly because it is a simple numbers game. You receive half of your DNA from your mom and the other half from your dad. No other relationship matches this closely. Once you expand beyond 2nd cousins, the amount of DNA you share with these relatives is significantly smaller. That is why most companies tell you that you are 3rd-5th cousins or something of the sort as the number of shared DNA segments decreases. Once you add in multiple lines of relationship, a 3rd cousin could actually be a 6th cousin through numerous lines. In short, the more DNA segments you have in common with another person, the better the testing companies are at determining your relationship to them.

So if your DNA indicates you are someone's son or daughter, you are their biological son or daughter. DNA does not lie.

You never see whites showing up with over 50% African or blacks with 99% European ethnicities, or something similar. However, I notice that AncestryDNA stopped showing the continent percentages, and now reports specific population groups. Are they trying to DE-racialize the results because customers are interpreting these continent categories in racial terms?

It might have less to do with race relations and more to do with AncestryDNA's competitors. Other testing companies have advertising campaigns where they emphasize the number of population groups they have. I think 23andMe is the most honest in that they allow you to see what their estimate is with different confidence levels.

Nevertheless, I do not think any of the companies, including AncestryDNA, explain precisely what the ethnicity/admixture results do and don't mean. People want to know where they are from and ethnicity results make answering the question simple. Not necessarily accurate, but simple.

On AncestryDNA I have distant cousins listed with their family tree with numerals to the right. Some are high 6 or 7, while others are low. What do the numbers indicate?

Those numbers indicate how many people in their tree share a particular surname. If you click on the number, then you will view a list of the individuals. You can use the surname list to compare to your known family names.

If Family Tree DNA is the only company that tests the Y-DNA, does it do any good to have a male test through AncestryDNA?

Family Tree DNA offers a Y-DNA STR test along with the newer Big Y SNP test. AncestryDNA also performs a truncated SNP test, although you only can see the results in the raw file, not on their website.

Y-DNA testing is only useful if you have a specific male line genealogical problem, such as the father of the father of your father is unknown. Autosomal testing is where you will find all of the cousins. Testing males or females through AncestryDNA's autosomal test is beneficial to locate cousin matches throughout all lines about 5-6 generations back in time. Additionally, Ancestry's database is roughly ten times the size of Family Tree DNA's Family Finder database.

AncestryDNA ethnicities are too uncertain. My friend tested with them, and one of his ethnicities showed up as Italy/Greece. Why would they combine Italian and Greek as one ethnicity?

Historically ample intermixing occurred among peoples along the Mediterranean Sea. On a chromosome level, it is difficult to distinguish between Greek and Italian with the limited reference populations that AncestryDNA has.

I would not characterize the uncertainty of ethnicities a bad thing. All of the testing companies ethnicity estimates are just that, estimates. The ambiguity is more a reflection of how human populations have spread throughout the world. We rarely cluster solely within our clan.

AncestryDNA is a private Mormon company head-quartered in Utah, USA, and partners with Family Search, an organization that wholly belongs to the Latter Day Saints ("Mormon") church. AncestryDNA shares its database with the Mormon church's "Family Search" organization. As such, you can end up baptized as a Mormon by your descendants after your death.

While Ancestry has several executives that are members of the Mormon church, The Church of Jesus Christ of Latter-Day Saints does not own it. A couple of private equity companies who have never had ties to the Mormon church (one is based in London and the other in San Francisco) own Ancestry LLC.

The Ancestry partnership with FamilySearch is identical to the relationship that FamilySearch has with MyHeritage, Find My Past, and American Ancestors. FamilySearch allows searching (and to a limited extent sharing) of each company's microfilmed record databases.

Ancestry does not share its DNA database with FamilySearch. In fact, there is no DNA record matching available on the FamilySearch Family Tree.

While the Mormon church claims a membership of 15 million, based on statistics from FamilySearch, the actual number of Mormons involved in family history research is less than 5% (about 750,000, worldwide). While Ancestry does not ask your religion, I suspect that the vast majority of the 7+ million people in their DNA database are not Mormon.

Almost all of the people in the AncestryDNA database are living. The FamilySearch Family Tree has more than 1 billion names in it of which 300-500 million are probably unique people. So the names in the Ancestry database are a small fraction of the names that FamilySearch already has recorded.

Currently, any proxy baptisms for those whom the Mormon church has forbidden (i.e., Jewish Holocaust victims and celebrities) can be reported, and the member of the church who performed that baptism will have their access to the FamilySearch website revoked. This action will curtail their ability to do any more proxy baptisms. There are also software controls in place to deny restricted names when anyone enters them the system. Any further attempts at circumventing these controls when found out by the church could subject the member to church discipline which may result in being disfellowshipped or excommunicated.

23ANDME

Does 23andMe have a Y-DNA test?

They do. The 23andMe genetic test includes a Y-DNA test. However, their Y test does not examine the same genetic attributes as the Family Tree DNA Y tests. 23andMe looks at SNPs while Family Tree DNA looks at STRs.

23andMe seems to have the most tools: chromosome browser, ancestral timeline, phasing with par-

ents, etc. What are the negatives of the 23andMe website?

The major weakness in 23andMe is that you have to opt-in to everything separately, from sharing your genealogical data to each health report.

23andMe is also not a genealogically driven company. The results page may display hundreds of matches, but only a fraction of the individuals have opted to share their genealogical data. I can find potential relatives, but determining how they fit in my family tree takes substantial effort.

How accurate is the 23andMe health info? If the data is not valid or useful, then the extra expense does not seem worth the cost especially if it might lead someone to become unnecessarily upset about an unrealistic health concern.

The study of DNA for health insight is in its infancy. The bigger question is, how much does your DNA influence the reported health attributes? 23andMe does a great job of providing you this information as well as referencing the applicable scientific reports.

An alternative genetic health service is Promethease.com. It offers a more comprehensive examination of the genetic health literature but lacks the interpretative data that 23andMe provides. With Promethease, you are on your own to slog through the research reports.

As with almost all cases, DNA is not a crystal ball predicting with certainty your health outcomes. There are numerous other factors, such as family history, environment, and gestational issues, which may play a more significant role in health issues.

That being said, I believe that knowledge is power. 23andMe gives you more insight. If you are afraid of what you will find out, then do not have your DNA tested for medical information.

23andMe has the largest reference populations and reports ethnicities based on confidence levels, unlike other companies. These are the MOST accurate results for me, but no company can give you precise results.

Agreed. Although MyHeritage DNA and Living DNA do not provide exact figures, it is believed that 23andMe's reference population contains the largest number of samples. Even then, only the European component has several thousand in the reference population. The Oceania population has less than 50.

I like the confidence level indicator, although for my results it does not change my makeup a whole lot.

23andMe MAKES MORE MONEY selling our genetic information to pharmaceutical research. Yes, they ask for your permission, but if they are making money from selling it should I be reimbursed for the money I spent giving them my DNA?

Since 23andMe is not a publicly traded company and they have not released detailed financial information, there is no available information to corroborate or refute the notion that 23andMe makes more money from selling the information than they do from selling the kits.

I have no problem with 23andMe making money on selling the collective data. They provided me with more than I gave them in dollars.

First, they took my DNA and sequenced it.

Second, they polled me for information about my medical history.

Third, they matched that information up with millions of other customers.

Fourth, they have identified potential areas of research based on the available literature.

All I did was pay $99, and I still got the raw DNA file. I also have access to tools for genealogical matching. By the way, these resources are part of my kit fee, unlike the upgrade charged by Family Tree DNA who does not sell your information. So the testing and reporting must be worth the $99.

There is nothing stopping anyone from attempting to sell their raw file to some pharmaceutical company. Don't be surprised when the company turns you down because it is not worth anything by itself.

FAMILY TREE DNA

How do you know that Family Tree DNA has the best tools for genealogical research?

Reading blogs, talking with people at conferences, listening to presentations, and trying out the tools for myself.

Family Tree DNA now accepts imported data from the other services. Wouldn't that make their database potentially the best overall?

Accepting imports and receiving them are two different things. Family Tree DNA allows you to filter out imported kits, and what I have found is that only about 10% of the database is imported data. Even though they have permitted imported data for years, their database has not increased in size significantly from transferred raw files. GEDmatch, on the other hand, has a database comparable in size to Family Tree DNA, and since they do not do testing, all of their data is made up of imports.

MYHERITAGE DNA

Would you recommend testing with MyHeritage DNA?

I recommend all of the major genealogical testing companies. It is wise to be in as many genetic genealogy matching pools as possible. You never know where your cousin connections will appear.

As of January 2018, MyHeritage DNA just passed the one million samples mark, only because they joined the competition in 2017. They permit transferring your AncestryDNA, 23andMe, or Family Tree DNA files to their database, so I expect it to grow as more people upload.

Will MyHeritage DNA always be the smallest genetic testing company?

If one genetic genealogy company has grown more than any other in 2017, it is MyHeritage DNA. MyHeritage increased from a few tens of thousands in their database to more than 1 million in one year. They are already comparable in size to Family Tree DNA, and within a couple of years, I suspect they may surpass 23andMe.

As a side note, I started 2017 with about 20 or so matches in the MyHeritage DNA database. By the middle of January 2018, I had over 2,500.

OTHER COMPANIES

Why haven't you reviewed National Geographic?

National Geographic is not valuable as a personal genomic indicator unless you are transferring data to Family Tree DNA. Their focus is on a broad population level of information, so they are distinctly different from the genealogical DNA testing companies. They do not have any capabilities to match with individuals which are a primary purpose of the genealogical DNA testing companies.

National Geographic's Genographic Project was one of the first genetic testing companies (launching in 2005). Now they claim the ability to pinpoint some of our origins thru GPS Origins™. Is this true?

I have not delved into this project much. From a genealogical standpoint, National Geographic does not allow you to match with others, so their test has limited use, regardless of the origin pinpoint claim.

From a scientific standpoint, the GPS Origins is an admirable project for understanding population migration. It combines genetic research with an ancestral tracking technique called Geographic Population Structure (GPS) to pinpoint more precisely where DNA originated. You can see how humans have developed over millennia by examining not only DNA, but also language, culture, and historical records (which National Geographic has done well for 100+ years).

However, I have the same criticism of the NatGeo project as with other companies about the admixture results they provide to individuals. Humans have migrated more often than the GPS Origins assumptions use to calculate admixture includes. The GPS Origins is accurate at a continental or regional level, but they are indeterminate at a country or smaller designation.

Living DNA declares it has the largest global database. It also provides the Y-DNA and mtDNA haplogroups. They even claim to pinpoint what country of origin. Is this company too good to be true?

As of January 2018, Living DNA has not released detailed information about their database size, but no other testing company has released such specific data either. It is hard to imagine that any company could claim they have the largest <insert sub group> breakdown.

If you want to match with other relatives, database size is the essential determining factor when selecting a genetic testing company. AncestryDNA wins that battle, as all companies have revealed how many DNA samples their databases contain.

The next key factor is the ability to match with other genetic kin. Living DNA does not provide any capability to find relatives, much like National Geographic. As such, it has minimal value from a genealogical perspective. Living DNA has stated they will add this feature at some point in 2018. If they do, then I would reevaluate my opinion.

Living DNA also claims the ability to pinpoint where in Britain your ancestors originated. I am skeptical of these claims until I have had a chance to research their methodology more. They claim twice as many ethnicity group delineations, but without more detail on the reference populations they use, I could not give an informed evaluation. Based on the ethnicity results of the other companies and having read extensively about their methodology, I do not put too much credence beyond continental level ethnic origins.

What about Oxford Ancestors for testing?

Oxford Ancestors only performs Y and Mitochondrial DNA testing. Without autosomal testing, they can provide limited genealogical information. It is also worth noting that when the founder of Oxford Ancestors, Professor Bryan Sykes, toured the US, he used 23andMe for testing and not his own company. 23andMe provides information on autosomal, Y-DNA, and mtDNA all in one test. Oxford Ancestors may compete with Family Tree DNA in Y-DNA testing; however, the company is virtually unknown outside of Great Britain. I would opt for Family Tree DNA or 23andMe over Oxford Ancestors.

What about the website www.accu-metrics.com?

Accu-Metrics has a different focus than the genealogy DNA testing companies reviewed in this book. This business focuses on establishing paternity, testing genetic disorders (such as Alzheimer), and testing hair for evidence of drug or alcohol.

Accu-Metrics does not provide any tools for genealogy minded people. If you are interested in genealogy and how your DNA fits in with others, you are better off going with one of the four major testing companies.

GEDMATCH

What does GEDmatch do that 23andMe does not?

GEDmatch allows you to compare your DNA results with people who have tested at different companies but have then uploaded their raw files to one central database. If you test with AncestryDNA and a relative tested at 23andMe, Family Tree DNA, or MyHeritage DNA, you can not compare your results without the third-party database such as GEDmatch.

GEDmatch has the best set of research tools that are more useful for comparing matches than 23andMe (one of which is chromosome phasing). Unfortunately, it is not the most user-friendly experience, but if you overlook that shortfall, the resources are fantastic.

Moreover, everyone you match with on GEDmatch is automatically in sharing mode. For 23andMe, each person has to opt-in to share.

Why does GEDmatch have a better ethnic breakdown than the other sites that more closely reflects what I understand about my family background?

For admixture, GEDmatch has more than a dozen different calculators designed with specific types of people in mind. Each of other the testing companies only use a single admixture calculator.

That being said, all of the GEDmatch calculators suffer from the same deficiencies as the testing companies ethnicity estimates.

My son took an AncestryDNA test, and I put the results on GEDmatch. I have not received emails from any possible cousin matches from GEDmatch. Since then, I took the DNA test. I have not put my results on GEDmatch in fear I did something wrong with my son's test. What do you think?

Perhaps you misspelled your email which is why no one is contacting you. Check your account settings. If you cannot log in because you have forgotten the password or the email, then try a different approach.

Upload your AncestryDNA results to GEDmatch. You should closely match your son on GEDmatch. Find out what the account email is for your son's DNA and then you can contact the owners of GEDmatch by email and see if they can help regain access to his account.

Another reason you are not receiving cousin connection emails it that your son is not a close enough match for people to reach out. By adding your DNA to GED-match, you create two reference points for people to match. This might increase your possible connections.

HEALTH REPORTS

If I wanted to transfer my DNA results from Family Tree DNA to 23andMe, could I have 23andMe only test for the health aspect, or would I have to buy a complete 23andMe test for that?

First, 23andMe does not accept transfers, so you can not transfer your results from Family Tree DNA to their company.

Next, to access the 23andMe health information you have to pay for one of their genetic+health assessment tests. Additionally, you have to opt-in to the health assessment results, or they will not reveal the results for which they tested.

Since you are interested in the health information and have taken a test with Family Tree DNA, you should investigate an alternative. For $5, Promethease.com will provide you similar health information. Keep in mind, that the low price generates the reports but isn't invested in a user-friendly experience like 23andMe has.

Keep in mind that Family Tree DNA has stated that their SNP selection was specifically made to exclude any sensitive health information. This restriction might put a limit on the amount of detail your Promethease reports provide. For $5, exploring Promethease as an alternative to the 23andMe test is worth investigating.

We want to use 23andMe for genetic and medical info and AncestryDNA for a better breakdown of heritage. Your suggestions?

If you have the money, pay the $199 for the 23andMe test. Then with your next $69-89 pay for an AncestryDNA test. You can then transfer your AncestryDNA data to Family Tree DNA and be able to use all of their tools for $19. Additionally, you can also obtain a Promethease report (with either 23andMe or AncestryDNA) for $5 to receive additional health/medical information.

I am looking for a company that can provide a kit for both Heritage+Health, like the one on 23andMe, but one that ships internationally.

You can always use Promethease.com for health. It costs about $5 or $10 and can use the raw file from any kit. AncestryDNA and MyHeritage DNA ships to many international destinations.

One limitation may be the country you are in and whether the laws prohibit personal DNA testing. If you travel at all, you might have a kit shipped to where you are visiting, and do the testing in that country. You should still be able to access your data over the internet.

WHICH TEST SHOULD I CHOOSE

All I want is an ethnic breakdown but being contacted by a relative would be cool. Which company should I choose, AncestryDNA or MyHeritage DNA?

If all you want is an ethnic breakdown, any company will work. What you could do is buy the AncestryDNA kit and then upload it to MyHeritage DNA. Then you can see how two different companies calculate your ethnicity.

Which company do you think is best?

"Best at what" is the real question? My personal favorite is 23andMe, but part of that is because I tested when they offered all of their health and trait reports using the V3 chip which had 900,000 SNPs, more than any other company.

However, AncestryDNA currently has the largest database. If you are trying to find people, DNA is a numbers game, and sizeable numbers tend to win out.

Family Tree DNA is a genealogist's company, particularly for their Y-DNA and mtDNA groups. They excel in these genetic communities.

MyHeritage DNA is new to the scene and growing. I'll watch them in 2018 to see how they improve their product and services.

Each company has their strengths. You would have to be more specific about what you are looking for to classify one of them as "the best."

Between best tools and largest pool of people who have taken the tested is 23andMe the best?

Actually, AncestryDNA has a database 2-3 times size of 23andMe. Family Tree DNA has a better array of tools and an engaged community of genetic researchers who usually reply to you when you have match questions. 23andMe has informative health reports and helps further medical research. Each company has pros and cons, which makes a "Best" designation misleading.

It seems like AncestryDNA has the best specific location results, countries vs. just continents; however, 23andMe has more detailed analysis. With that in mind, do third-party websites, like GEDmatch, provide better location information?

"Best" is a subjective term. AncestryDNA may have the ethnic classifications, especially in some regions of the world. However, I would not suggest that any of the companies have the best results. The data backing up their determinations (reference population sets) is not a large enough sample size or fidelity to claim any of the companies is the best.

With that in mind, I look at all of the location information with a grain of salt. There would be very little genealogical value to it unless you knew absolutely nothing about your ancestry, such as adoptees.

Which test will allow me to see my parent's ethnicities and view my genetic inheritance on a chromosome level?

23andMe is the only testing company that will do most of what you want, but you need to have at least one of your parent's test in addition to yourself.

You can do something similar on GEDmatch.com, but it is a little more complicated. You need to create phased kits for yourself using your parents' data and then run the Admixture tools on each of the phased kits.

No testing company analyzes down to a gene level. So you would need to have some knowledge of genes or use a website like SNPedia to map out specific genes on your chromosomes.

Is it possible to send two samples, one of my mother and one of myself, to the same company under one account?

Yes, if you use 23andMe. Under my 23andMe account, I manage more than 20 samples from grandparents to children to in-laws, and so on. Having a parent and child kit linked allows for some phased matching so that you can separate out what line (either your mother or your father's) the match is on. Also, having a parent and child kit makes forming triangulation groups easier, because you just need to find people that match both the parent and child.

You can access multiple kits using MyHeritage DNA as well. Family Tree DNA and AncestryDNA require separate logins for each test, although they have ways you can designate someone else as the manager.

For a male orphan, who has no information about their parents or grandparents, which company do you recommend using to try to trace from what part of the world his parents originate?

23andMe. For $99 or less the male orphan will receive his Y and mt haplogroups, which will tell him a bit about his paternal and maternal lines. The test also includes autosomal DNA which will give his a rough breakdown of your overall heritage/admixture/ethnicity. He can then transfer his tests to GEDmatch.com (for free), MyHeritage DNA (free), and Family Tree DNA (for $19). His DNA will now be in multiple databases for possible relative connections, and have additional ethnicity estimates to fine tune his heritage.

TRANSFERING YOUR DNA

Can I transfer my test results from 23andMe to AncestryDNA?

Nope. 23andMe and AncestryDNA do not allow transfers into their databases.

From my own experience, only about 10% of the matches I have in the Family Tree DNA database were transferred, so it is not that popular. On the other hand, as of late 2017, the GEDmatch.com database was 750,000 and growing by about 1,000 per day.

Does it cost money to transfer a kit? If so, how much?

Transferring to MyHeritage DNA is free. Transferring to GEDmatch is free. Uploading your raw DNA files to Family Tree DNA is initially free, but costs $19 to access their tools.

How do I upload my test kits from AncestryDNA and 23andMe to MyHeritage DNA?

Watch our YouTube Channel for instructions as we periodically make videos showing how to do this. In the meantime, be aware that each website keeps changing their procedures. The critical link you want to look for is "Raw Data" or "Raw File." Downloading this should result in a file that is between 5-15 MB. Use each website's search function to find the current instructions on how to download and upload files.

Seems like, if you have the money that Family Tree DNA testing is the way to go. From there, since AncestryDNA has the larger database, could you upload your file to them?

AncestryDNA does not accept uploads. So I would do it the other way. Test through Ancestry and then your results to Family Tree DNA. If you want the Y or Mt DNA tests, do those through Family Tree DNA, but unless you have a specific brick wall that you are working on that Y-DNA or mtDNA will help, then it will not be much help to you genealogically.

I uploaded one of my kits into GEDmatch.com how can I tell which one that was? I would like to upload both Ancestry.com and 23andMe kits.

GEDmatch kit numbers give you clues to which company processed the DNA. The letter in the kit number will identify the testing company. Just remember the acronym MATH:

M - 23andMe

A - AncestryDNA

T - Family Tree DNA

H - MyHeritage DNA

PRIVACY ISSUES

How will the DNA information be used? Can the companies doing these tests be trusted to preserve our privacy? What's to stop a hacker accessing the database?

The primary use for these companies is genealogical research by those individuals who have access to the matching database. Some of the companies, 23andMe most notably, sell the DNA database information to third parties for research, and they disclose this information in their terms and conditions.

In the Information Age, no company can guarantee your privacy. In the last couple of years, we have seen major high tech companies, big-name retailers, online dating sites, and even the IRS have their data breached. In some cases, exposing upwards of 100 million people by a single data breach. What is essential is that each business or organization have internet security protocols in place so that they can protect their customer's information.

DNA information is very low on the priority of interest for nefarious hackers. Someone breaking into a DNA database would have some names and birthdates and email addresses, any or all of which could be fabricated. Hacking a genetic genealogy database is not like breaking into a bank database which has more valuable information. Hackers would be far more interested in the name, address, and credit card number that is on file with the subscription side of the DNA businesses.

While the future may hold technology or innovation that will make DNA data more valuable, it is not right now. I find it informative that some of the most educated people in genetic genealogy have no problem posting all of their genetic information for anyone to use.

The problem with fearing unknown consequences is they are unknown. There are plenty of other things in life to fear that is known.

If privacy and security is a worry for you, then do not take a DNA test. If you have already tested but do not want a genetic company to keep the information, contact their customer service department to have your sample destroyed and your account deleted from their servers.

Could DNA test information be used in a criminal proceeding?

The chain of custody would not hold up in a court of law. If you submit a sample to a genetic testing company, you can indicate it belongs to whomever you want. Gathering any medical evidence for the judicial process involves multiple layers of checking, third-party witnesses to any events, and a paper trail for every step of the process. None of the consumer testing companies have anything close to that. Any halfway decent defense attorney would be able to have the evidence thrown out.

Google owns 23andMe. If you do not mind giving your DNA to the biggest data gathering conglomerate on the planet, who then gives all that info to the government without your knowledge or consent, then help yourself.

One of the founders of 23andMe was married to one of the founders of Google. They have since divorced but are still on speaking terms and run a non-profit together. Since 23andMe is a privately held company, they do not have to disclose who their owners/investors are.

While Google did invest $3.6 million in 23andMe during the early stages, there have been hundreds of millions invested since then. Google does not report 23andMe in their SEC filings as one of their investments. To assert that Google owns 23andMe is pure speculation without any supporting evidence.

Horror stories circulate about the government accessing genetic test database and finding family members of people taking a DNA test that may have committed crimes. Which company cares the most about confidentiality and privacy and will not give other people access to your information while allowing you to know about your background? Do any laws prevent companies from releasing your DNA?

First, I have only heard of one instance where police were involved in trying to obtain information from a genealogy DNA company. If I remember the details correctly, they had a warrant, and what they found was inconclusive. The genealogy testing companies are not a good source of DNA for the court system because there is no chain of custody like there would be when gathering evidence. In other words, the only reason 23andMe tags my sample as mine is because I said it was my sample. No court of law will accept that as evidence. The prosecutor would have to show proof that I might have committed the crime, then obtain a court order to receive a DNA sample from me (with proper chain of custody). At which point, what good was the genealogy DNA sample? None. The prosecutor has my DNA from the court ordered test.

Next, all of the companies care about your confidentiality and privacy. It is good business. However, all of them use your results for their internal research and algorithmic development. Some companies sell anonymized sample sets to outside parties for research. The Genetic Information Nondiscrimination Act of 2008 protects you from being denied insurance because of a DNA sample.

Finally, several attorneys that are also genetic genealogists (for instance Judy Russell or Blaine Bettinger) could speak better to these legal issues. However, they are not a concern to the point that they recommend not testing.

How can you be sure this is not a scam?

Having tested with multiple companies and seeing the genetic matches being the same, should be evidence enough that it is not a scam. Stick with the major firms (AncestryDNA, 23andMe, Family Tree DNA and MyHeritage DNA) if you are concerned about being scammed.

What if I had to give a DNA sample as part of a criminal proceeding? Can I use that to match with other people?

My guess is they probably are not going to release your DNA to you. Additionally, the criminal DNA test analyzes different segments of your genome. The results will not be much help in matching family members.

If you want to see how you are related to others, then you will still need to test through one of the genealogical testing companies.

What happens if these sites are hacked? How do these sites protect your data and privacy from being leaked and abused?

I do not know the specifics of any companies data security. Research the companies individually to determine their protocols. Be advised; US laws protect you from insurance companies using your DNA to make coverage decisions.

Will the companies send my genetic information to the government?

There has been no evidence presented that any of the genealogical testing companies are sending our results to the government. While 23andMe may have received some grant money for research from the federal government, I am not aware of any government funding of AncestryDNA, MyHeritage DNA, or Family Tree DNA. However, 23andMe has not sent individual DNA to the governments that provided funding for research, only anonymized DNA test sets based on specific research criteria.

Can Google use your data to send you targeted ads based on your genetic makeup?

Perhaps, but unlikely since there is very little genetic information that would be applicable to advertising. If this is a concern, use a separate email for your DNA accounts. I use a dedicated DNA email with all of the sites. In six years, I have never had any ads or spam sent to that email address.

Matching & Inheritance

A genealogist told me that misattributed paternity is likely to happen the further back in time you go. Is this true?

A genetic expert indicated that misattributed paternity is likely to happen the further you investigate into the past. Is this true?

Misattributed paternity or a non-paternity event (NPE) is a real thing. It boils down to the father listed on the birth record not being the biological father. An NPE is not the same thing as being adopted or having no father listed.

There have been numerous NPE studies conducted, and their results indicate the rate of occurrence ranging from less than 1% to as high as 10%. This NPE rate varies across cultures and time periods.

I wholeheartedly agree that it happens. DNA testing has revealed some relationships in my research that can only be explained by NPE. The likeliness of it happening over time is a simple matter of mathematics. By multiplying each generation by the NPE probability, we can determine the likelihood that all of the genealogical links are correct. Depending on what the rate of NPE is, the possibility being 50% accurate could occur in just a few generations.

Review the table below for the probability that every link in a chain of people back to some number of generations for an ancestor is correct:

	Rate of NPE				
Generations	**1%**	**2%**	**3%**	**5%**	**10%**
1	99%	98%	97%	95%	90%
2	98%	96%	94%	90%	81%
3	97%	94%	91%	86%	73%
5	95%	90%	86%	77%	59%
10	90%	82%	74%	60%	35%
15	86%	74%	63%	46%	21%
20	82%	67%	54%	36%	12%
25	78%	60%	47%	28%	7%

Let's use an example. On paper, you descend from William Bradford, who arrived on the Mayflower. He lived about 400 years ago, or around 15-20 generations back. What this table shows is that if the NPE rate throughout that time was 1%, then there is an 82%-86% chance that William Bradford is, in fact, your ancestor. On the other hand, if the NPE rate is 10%, then there is only a 12%-21% chance that you are related to William Bradford.

You will notice that the more generations you follow back in time, the lower the likelihood is that all the links are correct. You can calculate this yourself by using the formula

$P=(1-r)n$. Where P is the probability, r is the NPE rate, and n is the number of generations.

Which site is the most accurate in matching DNA with potential relatives?

Unlike ethnicity percentages, when it comes to how much we match with potential relatives, there is some hard data we can examine. Matching with family members is based on the amount of shared DNA. But not just any amount of DNA is considered a match; there is usually a threshold that each company uses based on cM and SNPs that have to the same to be considered a genealogically significant shared segment. All of the testing companies use somewhere around 10cM and/or 500-900 SNPs as the threshold for reporting shared segments.

If you compare match results from different companies (such as the same relatives in AncestryDNA, 23andMe, etc.), you will find that results for close matches the results are almost identical and distant family members have similar results. The variance between companies might result from:

1. Each company is testing a different set of SNPs and will have differing amounts of cM between each SNP.

2. Threshold rules to determine matching segments, while similar, are different between companies.

3. Chance misreads from the microarray chip may affect segment matches in rare instances.

The amount of difference in accuracy for matching segments between companies does not matter in a genealogical context. For example, you match a distant cousin but one company reports 87.5 cM shared and the other indicates 87.3 cM shared, you are still related to that distant cousin in the same way.

To identify which company is the most accurate regarding matching, you could set up an experiment. You would need to have a set of known relationships that span a significant genealogical time span (about 5-6 generations), and then have those people test at all of the different companies. This comparison is expensive. You will probably need around 50 related individuals times by $99 times by 5 companies = $25,000. You would also want to do a whole genome sequencing of each of these individuals for further comparison.

After all of this, I doubt that there would be a statistically significant difference between the companies. Use your money more efficiently by testing more people rather than the same people at multiple companies.

How far back in time can you match with someone?

Autosomal DNA matching is only reliable for the most recent 5-6 generations. After that, the fractions of DNA are so minuscule that they are mixed in with the randomness of being human and sharing 99.9% of your DNA with everyone else.

Y-DNA or mtDNA can match much further back, but those are only on your patrilineal or matrilineal lines.

While you may match someone nine generations back and figure out your most recent common ancestor (I have done this), that is purely a matter of luck (because of the randomness) and usually, involves both people having an extensive paper trail already established (we both did).

The only living males on my mother's side are my son and a first cousin. Which individual will give the best DNA results for my mother's side of the family?

Given that you are looking at males on your mother's side, it seems you are looking only for your mother's father's line. Your son would not have your mother's father's Y-DNA. A first cousin will only have your mother's father's DNA if the male is a son of your mother's brother. If he is, then the first cousin would have your mother's father's Y-DNA, but there is more to your mother's DNA than her father's Y-DNA.

Assuming your mother is deceased, YOU share the most DNA with her. Also, since autosomal testing does not discriminate between male and female, I would test yourself, any siblings of yours, and any siblings of your mother who are still living. Your son has less of your mother's DNA than you do. Your first cousin also has a different mixture of your mother's family's DNA than you do. Test the first cousin after you have tested your siblings and aunts and uncles but before you test your son.

To match with other people, I would use the AncestryDNA test first and the 23andMe test second.

ADOPTION CASES

My step-dad is adopted and trying to find his biological parents. Which DNA test would you recommend to help give him some leads?

For adoptees, there are usually two DNA tests that you can take which will give you leads. The first is a Y-DNA STR test which currently only Family Tree DNA offers. Since your step-dad is male, he will share the same Y-DNA with all of his direct male ancestors. The Family Tree DNA Y-DNA test may give surnames that are common to his Y-DNA profile. Additionally, he may match closely with others within a few generations. These results and matches can help focus his research on some families and areas in helping to determine who his father was.

The second type of test that is beneficial is an autosomal DNA test which all of the testing companies offer. This test can match you with ancestors from any of your family lines extending back about 5-6 generations. Testing or uploading to multiple genetic databases will increase the number of close relatives that might be discovered and help determine his parentage.

Once you have done both of these tests, you might also consider contacting one of the many genetic genealogists that specialize in adoption cases.

I was adopted and am female. I know my birth mother but not my birth father. Which DNA test would you suggest? All I have to go on is a name.

Unfortunately, Y-DNA testing is not going to help you, so you need to do an autosomal test. This test is the most common and any of the major companies sell one. Since you do not know anything about your father, you want to be in the biggest databases to have the highest probability of making close matches.

With the limited information you have, I would suggest AncestryDNA simply because it has the largest database. After you receive your results, transfer your raw data file to GEDmatch.com, Family Tree DNA, and MyHeritage DNA. If you have money for a second test, use 23andMe.

If your mother is willing, test her and then compare the matches you have with hers. To start finding potential paternal relatives, focus on the close matches you have that your mother does not match. Using the name that you have, you can search through your matches' online trees or ask them directly about any potential relatives. While it may not seem like much, having a name and knowing who your mother was will make searching for your father a less daunting task.

I am a female looking for my biological father about whom I have no information. I have two half-brothers, but they both have different fathers. I have tested with AncestryDNA, and I am in the process of testing my mother with them as well. I have also uploaded my results to MyHeritage DNA and will do the same with my mom's results as soon as they are available.

My matches on Ancestry all seem to link to my mother's line. My question is, am I wasting my time? Is there a chance that I can find relatives of my biological father this way or do you have any suggestions to improve my odds?

First thing, download your RAW files from AncestryDNA and transfer them to GEDmatch (for free) and Family Tree DNA (for a $19 fee per kit). By so doing, you will place your DNA in other databases and possibly match individuals who are not in the AncestryDNA database. Transferring your raw files improves your odds of making additional matches.

With your mother and your results on GEDmatch, you will be able to phase yourself, giving you one phased kit from your mother and one phased kit from your father. You can use this paternal phased kit for finding matches. Using a phased kit will eliminate the matches of your mother's side which may be more numerous and closely related.

Now whether you will find anyone depends on two factors.

1. First, whether or not there are any relatives out there. If your father came from families that only had 1 or 2 kids, there might be a handful of cousins to match to (my wife has this problem).

2. Second, paternal cousins will have to have taken a DNA test. As of the end of 2017, about 3% of the US population has tested. Consider this project as more of a long-term search plan.

My mother was adopted, and I do not know who my father is. I wanted to learn more about myself, so which DNA test would be best for me?

Choose AncestryDNA and 23andMe. They have the largest databases. Transfer your AncestryDNA over to Family Tree DNA and MyHeritage DNA so that you will be in all four databases. Then start contacting the close matches that you find.

Without any other close relatives, it will be hard to figure out to which side of the family your matches belong. Hopefully, there is a half-aunt/uncle or cousin that you match with that can give you a successful starting point.

INHERITED TRAITS & DNA

I am not so sure about the accuracy of these eye color results. On DNA.land, it suggested I should have brown eyes. GEDmatch.com said I should have blue. However, I have green eyes. Why don't the results align with what I have?

The results do not align because a significant number of genes are involved. Pigmentation (eye, hair, and skin color) are complex traits to predict. Take the test results as a plausible prediction, but not necessarily reality.

Also, recognize that blue and green are the same color for most of these genes. Additionally, eye color is much more than just a color; there are genes that code for rings, starbursts, and flecks all of which could be different hues impacting the color of your eyes.

I have one sister, and we do not physically resemble each other not much. Why are we so different?

Each person (other than identical twins) is a unique mixture of their parents' and their ancestors' DNA. We share approximately 50% of our DNA with siblings. This percentage helps explain why some siblings appear so similar. By contrast, we have 50% of our DNA that is different, which explains why some siblings seem like they are not related at all. Even with identical twins, there are environmental factors that act on their DNA making them appear different. In the end, we are all unique even though we share DNA.

My parents had seven kids, two girls and five boys. If we test each sibling, what is the chance that every piece of our parent's DNA can be captured?

Every piece? Extremely small but still possible. Although the more children tested, the closer to 100% DNA coverage you get. Siblings share sizeable amounts of DNA. As such, testing an additional child only adds a diminishing quantity of DNA from the parent's genome. One child has 50% of the total parental genome. Two children should cover 75% of the parental genome. Three children have 88%, four children have 93%, five children have 97%, six children have 98%, and seven children have 99%. After testing all of your siblings, 1% of your parents DNA might still be unaccounted for.

After seeing many DNA results, I find most of them are ridiculous. You can see the blackest people, and they have more European percentages than someone who looks completely white. How is that possible when your features and skin color show the opposite?

Since many genes for pigmentation are dominant, you can easily have a majority European heritage and still have dark skin. Likewise, if the luck of the draw gives you the lack of pigmentation genes from your few European ancestors you can have fair skin while being predominantly sub-Saharan African. DNA is random like that.

I read an article suggesting that sometimes a grandmother has a "favorite" grandchild, one with which she just seems to share a special bond. The premise of the article was that some grandchildren have more of the grandmother's DNA than her other grandchildren might have. The report claimed that these grandchildren are the female children of the grandmother's male children. Have you ever heard of this theory, and is there any validity to it?

I have not heard that theory, but you could attempt to determine who has more of grandma's DNA. You would need to test grandma to discover which of your siblings and you had the most. If grandma is deceased, there is no way to find out who got more at this point.

On average grandchildren share 25% of their autosomal DNA with each grandparent. However, the average is collective. Individually, it can range from 20%-30%. The excursions from 25% are not dependent on whether it is a paternal or maternal grandmother. I know that from having looked at DNA of hundreds of grandparent/grandchild pairs.

As a female, you would carry slightly more DNA from your paternal grandmother than your brothers, because you would also have an X chromosome that could trace back to that paternal grandmother. However, from an autosomal DNA standpoint, no mechanism gives girls more DNA from a particular grandparent.

The other problem with this theory is defining who the "favorite" grandchild is. Absent a confession from the grandparent or an in-depth observation of how the grandmother interacts with each of the grandchildren over an extended period; I am not sure how you would be able to define this.

RELATIONSHIPS REVEALED IN DNA

I have a question concerning cousins issued from identical twin brothers. My father is half of an identical twin pair. Would DNA from his twin brother make his children appear as though they are my half-siblings?

Yes! That is exactly what it would look like. So do not start any family feuds because of a mischaracterized relationship. Note that this false half-sibling relationship will carry on with each generation (so half-cousins, half-nephews, etc.).

What kinds of relationship would double first cousins most resemble?

Double first cousins share approximately 25% of their DNA with some of the segments being a full match. I have only seen a couple of examples of them and cannot draw any firm conclusions of general characteristics of their DNA. Grandparents, aunts/uncles, and nephews also share 25% of your DNA. However, double first cousins are the only 25% relationship that has full matching segments (but not near as much as siblings have).

How does endogamy affect our genetic relationships?

Endogamy is when a relatively small population interbreeds with little outside influence. Think of groups like the Amish or Ashkenazi Jews. Endogamy also happens in isolated communities like islands.

The primary effect of this interbreeding is that spouses might be related in multiple ways. Most societies shun sibling marriages, but first cousin unions are acceptable.

Over time, the DNA pool is limited, and many segments may be shared throughout the group. When comparing people from an endogamous population, you might notice full match segments and much more shared DNA than would be expected. For instance 6th cousins having the same amount of shared DNA as 4th cousins. This makes identifying the relationships without paper records particularly problematic.

Should I test my half-aunt? She is my grandma's child but not my grandpa's. Would her test results allow me to filter my matches and tell me who is from my grandma's side?

That is an excellent use of half-siblings for filtering results. Recognize though that your half-aunt only has a portion of your grandmother's DNA. What this means is that you will still have some matches that are on your grandmother's line which your half-aunt does not match. So use your half-aunt's results to confirm that a match is on your grandmother's side, but don't assume that a potential relative that does not match your half-aunt is on your grandfather's side.

My AncestryDNA test shows my uncle as a distant cousin. Why is that?

The results present a couple of possibilities:

1. By chance, DNA recombination has made it so that you and your uncle show much less than the 25% average shared DNA. Instead, you have shared segments amounting to the upper range of where a distant cousin shares.

2. He is, in fact, a half-uncle in which case his DNA would resemble a cousin match. A half-uncle would share only one of your grandparent's DNA.

Other explanations might exist. Unless you know that possibility 2 is a fact, then option 1 is probably more likely. If you have access to your parent's DNA, you can compare them to the uncle. Your parent should show up as a sibling for case 1, or a half-sibling for case 2. Most of the companies do not report half or double relationships because they are much rarer than full-relatives.

23andMe and AncestryDNA both indicate that a middle-aged woman is my first cousin and my dad's half-sister. These results make no sense because my dad does not have any half-siblings. What's going on?

The woman is your dad's half-sister and your half-aunt.

The DNA companies do not report half or double relationships beyond half-siblings because overlapping possibilities are too numerous. Half-aunts and cousins share approximately the same amount of DNA, so that is why your results indicate she is a cousin to you (rather than a half-aunt as I suggest). I have this same situation on some of the kits I manage.

It is possible, although highly unlikely, that this woman is more distantly related by a generation and on the high end of inheritance which makes it appear as a half-sibling.

However, I have never found a match on any of the companies databases that are reported as a half-sibling and then found out to be a first or second cousin, aunt, or uncle. These are the only relationships that are remotely possible to share the same amount of DNA as a half-sibling.

The probability she is your half-aunt (your dad's half-sister) is greater than 95%. With that amount of shared

DNA, there are only a few relationships that it could be, and two of them are grandparent or grandchild. Since she is middle-aged and your father knew his parents, you can discount that possibility. Since she is middle-aged, it precludes her from being your Dad's aunt. The most likely situation is that your dad did not know that he had a half-sibling. I think you may have uncovered a family secret.

If I share a small segment of DNA with my second cousin but not my dad, is it possible that my mother had a liaison with one of my dad's relatives (perhaps a brother or uncle) and I inherited slightly different DNA for that reason?

That might be a possibility if you could not compare your DNA directly with your father's. On a chromosome map, your father will be a half-match across all 22 chromosomes. Your father's brother or uncle would not be a half-match in every location, thus would share a significantly smaller amount of DNA with you.

The smaller the DNA segment you share with any match (including second cousins), the increased likelihood that is a false match. Random chance events cause the false matches because humans share 99.9% of their DNA.

Another possibility, is that you are related to your second cousin through your mother as well, although more distantly.

A likely case is there is a discrepancy in the analyzed SNPs from this DNA segment. Either through no calls, miscalls, or not even looking at the same SNPs. My grandfather and I had tested with the V3 chip from 23andMe, my father with the V4 chip from 23andMe, and our second cousin with the V1 chip from AncestryDNA. Each one of those uses a different set of SNPs although there is quite a bit of overlap between them.

So, the paternal relative liaison possibility is the least likely of several potential explanations.

On AncestryDNA, I recently had 2nd cousin matches changed to 3rd cousins. What happened that made the change?

The AncestryDNA's algorithm changed. Most likely they identified segments that were statistically too insignificant to be included and removed them. The new algorithm decreased the overall amount of shared DNA and the number of shared segments. As a result, AncestryDNA changed the relationship classification of your cousin.

Is it possible that some of our ancestors had relationships with multiple spouses and some of them might have been incestuous?

It is not only possible, but because of the number of people throughout history, it is almost a certainty. Identifying where that happened could be tricky. Autosomal DNA testing can only provide records for relationships 5-7 generations back. Non-paternity events (where the father is not the same as the one listed on a birth record) are easy to detect through direct testing. Siblings who appear as half-siblings rather than full siblings have one different parent, usually the father. However, NPEs are more difficult to decipher when comparing distant cousins. The range of shared DNA between 6th cousins overlaps with shared DNA between half-6th cousins. Thus causing confusion.

My uncle mentioned that an ancestor was a slave in the late 1700s/early 1800s. If so, this ancestor would appear as a 6th generational link (or maybe 7th). I do not have any identification of an African link on my Ancestry.com DNA results. Is that generational link one of the ones that you mentioned - i.e., only 50-95% likely to match with me?

Yes, 6th or 7th generation is the edge of where you can expect reliable DNA matches, and it actually has a much lower probability (around 1% of the people you are related to at 6th or 7th generation will share any DNA with you) of being found. So the vast majority of your slave ancestor's descendants won't share DNA with you.

If my brother had a test done, could he have different ancestors show up than me from the 6th and 7th generation?

Certainly. You and your brother will inherit some of the same DNA from your parents (about 50%), but you will also each inherit 50% that the other did not receive. In the 6th generation, there may be 1 or 2 ancestors out of 64 that you or your brother are not related to genetically. In the 7th generations, you will not inherit the genes of at least a half-dozen to two dozen ancestors.

I want to learn more about my father's line, but I do not know of close living relations that I can test. I have tested a first cousin and a great aunt on my mother's side of the tree. I thought I could filter out results from mom's line if a match did not match these maternal relatives. However, the results that do not match my maternal first cousin do match distant relations on my mother's side. How is that possible? Why can't I find my father's relations?

Matching without close known relatives can be tricky. Here are some things that everyone should keep in mind:

1. Multiple relationship paths - unrelated people can be related to the same person through different lines. For instance, I have one match to which my wife, my sister-in-law, and I are all related. Be aware, the three of us share no DNA between us; however, we all are related to this person through different genealogical lines.

2. False matches - when dealing with small segments (under 10cM) the likelihood increases of a match being false or having no actual genealogical connection.

3. Small families - families that only had one or two children for several generations did not leave abundant DNA to spread around and share with others. My wife was disappointed in her 23andMe results because there were not many possibilities she could match. My wife's paternal line were only children for three generations, and her maternal line had only a couple of children in each generation.

4. Database - you cannot match if your relatives are not in the same database as you. My wife's disappointment was turned around after she tested with AncestryDNA and there was a host of matches including some that helped her confirm research she had completed. I have had the opposite experience by having more closely related matches on 23andMe compared to Ancestry.

With this in mind, always use triangulation whenever matching to help identify common groups to whom you are related.

Recognize that great-aunts, first cousins, and your mother do not capture all of the DNA your common ancestors produced. You can have matches that share segments with your cousin or great-aunt and not match you or your mother, and still link into your maternal family line.

Additionally, your father might have shared more ancestry with your mother than previously known, which is why his line seems to be without matches.

Alternatively, your father's heritage falls into one of the caveats mentioned above.

Test or upload results to multiple databases. Unfortunately, there is not anything you can do to overcome the small family problem. More people are testing over time so if you have not found what you are looking for today, as with any other genealogical problem, revisit your results in a year and examine what new thing has popped up.

Ethnicity

ETHNICITY BASICS

What is the difference between genealogical matching and ethnicity?

Genealogical matching is using DNA results to find segments that are in common with other people. Multiple long segments of shared DNA indicate a closer relationship. Many people talk about this as finding or matching cousins.

Ethnicity is an estimate made by comparing your DNA sequences with those of reference sets that represent different historical populations. Groups can be as large as a continent or as small as a town. Ethnicity is also known as admixture or heritage.

Would I be able to determine my ethnicity if I took a paternity test at my doctor's office?

It depends on what is in the file and how big it is. The data would need the following:

1.   Contain SNP data - not every genetic test is going to be analyzing the raw SNP data.

2.   Contain information on all 23 pairs of chromosomes - most paternity tests only examine the Y-

DNA, which won't tell you much about your ethnicity.

3. Contain hundreds of thousands of SNPs - without enough data; there is no reliable way to use the different algorithms that have been set up to calculate ethnicity.

4. Be in a format that is uploadable to GEDmatch - if it is not, then you have scads of work to do. I would advise retyping 500,000 lines of information.

Paternity tests were designed to test for paternity. If it does something else, great, but don't count on it.

Stop being politically correct and use the word RACE...it is a biological reality.

All of the testing companies use "ethnicity," "admixture," or "heritage." These words imply some sub-classifications other than "race." Historically, western society classified people into three races (Negroid, Mongoloid, and Caucasian). However, ethnicity usually further divides these groups. For instance, Slavs, Anglo-Saxons, Scandinavians would all be considered part of the Caucasian race but are genetically different enough that we can identify their variants in DNA.

What DNA has shown is that there is a definite blurring of race/ethnicity particularly on the fringes of populations where intermixing has occurred. Since about 500 years ago, when transoceanic travel began, that intermixing has increased dramatically. My guess is if DNA testing had not been made affordable until 200 years from now, determining any ethnic or racial origins would be nearly impossible because of the increased intermingling that will occur over the next centuries. With 500 years of intermingling, determining specific ethnicity is already faulty.

Does each company have a different database of DNA to determine your ethnicity results?

Yes, each company has their own reference populations. The reference population is made up of people that meet the individual company's specific criteria, which usually includes three items:

1. All four grandparents are from the same area (country, region, etc.).

2. The area cannot be a country primarily populated by colonial immigrants (i.e., USA, Canada, Australia).

3. The sample cannot be closely related to someone who is already part of the reference population (i.e., you and your brother would not both be able to be included in the reference population).

Where did the initial 10,000 samples for the reference population originate?

Some of the reference population samples were involved in public research projects. Other reference population data derives from customers of each DNA testing company.

How do testing companies determine which ethnic groups to lump together, as they seem arbitrary? For example, why does one company group French and German together rather than French and Spanish?

The results from the testing companies are not arbitrary. Since the companies are marketing to ordinary people, they chose to use country names to classify the majority of their groupings. The ancestry groups were teased out, and then each company had to given the subsets a name.

There is much rationale behind the decision to name each group. From what we know of history (and geography), there was more intermixing of the people in the areas of France and Germany than there was between the peoples of Spain and France. So lumping France and Germany together makes historical sense that the data appears to support the grouping.

If you are interested, 23andMe has a white paper explaining how they made these selections. It is available on their website.

ACCURACY

How seriously should we take the DNA tests? Should they be taken with a pinch of salt?

For ethnicity, yes. The ethnicity results are rough estimates, and there are many reasons why it may not reflect what you expect based on your paper research.

The raw data results (the ACGT reading of your SNPs) however are 99.99%+ accurate.

I do not care about my family history; I only want to know to which ethnicity I belong.

Unfortunately, DNA is not going to be able to answer your question with any degree of accuracy right now. However, take the test. Perhaps the reference populations in the future will be accurate enough to give a high level of confidence of your ethnicity.

Despite testing a lot of different markers, can genetic testing companies still only determine your ethnicity with only 0.1% margin of error?

First, no company claims they can determine your ethnicity with only a 0.1% error margin. Most will report results down to 0.1%, but if you dig into their literature, they will also tell you that anything below 1%-5% could just be noise and probably isn't accurate.

Next, it is important to understand that there is a difference between "accuracy" and "precision." Accuracy is related to the ability to determine the correct answer. From a genealogical standpoint, if ethnicity results were accurate, then they would line up with the results found through a paper trail.

Precision is related to the ability to reproduce the same or very similar answer when doing the same process repeatedly. In other words, if each company took your same sample and tested it multiple times, the results should be nearly identical.

Reporting ethnicity results to 0.1% is a hallmark of precision. All of the companies are precise. They have run your sample through their algorithms and checked and cross-checked for errors, hence the precision.

No testing company has provided reliable data that they are accurate at their smallest reported ethnicity levels.

Some testing companies report ethnicities from the continental to regional and country levels. Are any of them accurate?

Ethnicity results are based on a mathematical formula to examine modern people and make an estimate of where those people's DNA relatives lived several generations ago.

Having reviewed the results of numerous people who have tested with different companies, I can confidently state that the results at the continental level are accurate. Some of the regional gradations are accurate, mainly in Europe, but it varies by company. This accuracy is due to the size of their reference databases. Theoretically, the more samples in the database, the higher the degree of accuracy On a country or smaller level, very little data supports the reported results with a high degree of certainty.

Why did I receive vastly different ethnicity results when I uploaded my AncestryDNA results to GEDmatch.com and MyHeritage DNA?

The varying ethnicity results are not unexpected. Each company tests a different set of SNPs and has their own algorithm and reference population with which to compare DNA. If the results were the same, then I would suspect they were using the same algorithm and reference database.

AncestryDNA gives probability ranges one level deeper (like the average was 33% British but the probability range is from 5% to 70%). How does the probability scale affect accuracy?

23andMe also has a way to play with the confidence level to display your ethnicity percentages. The problem I see with this mathematical manipulation is increased misinterpretation because most people lack an understanding of statistical applications.

A report could claim a 95% certainty that the range is between 5% and 70%. In simplified language, you have somewhere between one and twelve great-grandparents who are from Great Britain (or whose ancestors were primarily from Great Britain). With that large of a range, it is hard to be wrong.

Sad to see so many of the comments are about ethnicity results. This is the least useful reason to take the DNA test.

DNA can be complicated, and it takes a bit of learning to understand. However, the usefulness of the ethnicity results decreases if a sizeable database to match with is lacking. If populations were isolated for a long enough time, figuring out the ethnicity would be a cinch. Researchers can easily tell the difference between modern humans, Neanderthals, Denisovans, and other archaic humans. However, these were isolated groups with only minimal interbreeding and in limited geographic locations. A few hundred thousand years of isolation made their DNA easily distinguishable.

For modern humans, the majority of the continents' populations remained isolated from each other for tens of thousands of years. Ethnicity results reflect this historical fact. Within a continent like Europe, it is moderately easy to detect the difference between the Slavs and the British. However, as you observe Germans and Swedes, the noticeable differences diminish.

Theoretically, if researchers had a sizeable reference population supported by reliable paper records differentiating populations, then ethnicity testing could be considered accurate. However, to obtain that level of accuracy, millions of unrelated people have to have researched their ancestry.

I consider the ethnicity results as a marketing gimmick. The marketing gimmick is what sells the tests, without which there will not be an improvement of the reference databases.

Because everyone invaded Britain, English DNA would have all those tribes that cheerfully invaded the UK, including Scotland, Ireland, and even Wales. Why are the ethnicity results not reflecting this historical fact?

Historical realities are what makes the testing companies walk a fine marketing line. IF they told everyone in explicit terms what the ethnicity really meant (including accuracy and repeatability figures), it would bore everyone to death, and no one would buy their product.

The real value in DNA testing is the genealogical matching NOT the ethnicity. Unfortunately, the tests are marketed primarily as an ethnicity test since it is much easier to understand that you are part Russian, part Middle Eastern and part East Asian. However, companies have to make money otherwise there wouldn't be the test data to match genealogically.

Are people expecting too much from DNA testing? The reporting of SNP reads and haplogroups is very accurate. Does the primary problem pertain to lack of understanding geographical/ethnic results?

Yes. People's expectations, particularly how much emphasis they place on ethnicity results, needs to change. That happens by sharing the message and educating people. Part of those expectations are from the fact that this is new technology, and part of those expectations are from the DNA testing company's marketing messages.

My brother and I sent our samples to AncestryDNA recently. We have the same biological parents, but our results were significantly different. For example: 60% vs 35% Scandinavia, 13% vs 0% Iberian Peninsula, 2% vs 46% Great Britain. Based on these results, isn't genetic testing no better than astrology?

How companies determine your relationships and how they define an ethnic makeup (or admixture) are two very different processes and algorithms.

The relationship process is very straightforward, scientifically sound, and repeatable across companies. You are comparing the total amount of shared DNA and shared segments. AncestryDNA probably identified you two as siblings even before you linked yourselves to a tree. DNA can do that for close relationships (up to 2nd cousins) almost perfectly. Half- and double-relationships can muddy the waters, but there aren't many of those overall.

However, for the ethnicity makeup, companies have to process small segments of your DNA and classify them into whichever categories they have. On average, you share about 50% of your DNA with your brother, which means that 50% is different. As such, it is highly likely that you have different ethnicity makeups because of the 50% you each don't have.

The admixture results are only as reliable as the database of reference populations that each company has. A database would need to have a reference population set in the millions, which is a long way off, to be truly reliable.

Since brothers do not share the same DNA, is it possible to have a 100% Irish parent and a 100% Italian parent to pass on ethnicities where one son is an Irish/Italian mix, and the other is 100% Irish?

No, you receive 50% of your DNA from your mother and 50% from your father. So you and your brother would both be an Irish/Italian mix. While it is theoretically possible to inherit a completely different 50% from your mother and father than your brother, statistically this on the order of 1 chance in trillions. For all practical purposes, that equates to zero percentage likelihood. Brothers would have an Irish/Italian mix. If a brother did turn up with a 100% of either ethnicity, the parents were not fully Irish or Italian.

Is MyHeritage DNA accurate? They insist that because they have 52 reference populations that they are the most accurate. Is this true?

No, they have the most reference populations, but that does not prove the samples sizes of the reference sets are the largest. No company can determine who is most accurate. When they report ethnicity estimates, there are so many variables that accuracy beyond the continental level is sketchy in all but a few instances.

One minor group that does distinguish itself from others genetically is the Ashkenazi Jews. The reason is that the Ashkenazis have primarily married within their own community. Additionally, this group was a pioneer in having their population involved in genetic testing for medical reasons.

I am picturing a few guys in a warehouse puffing on cigars, randomly picking out Ping-Pong balls from one of those bingo rotary things, and just assigning whatever to whomever.

While that is a funny image, I know just enough about math to be able to state it is not the case. If your scene were the case, I would expect vastly differing results from my brothers and I. There were slight differences, but all of our tests put as at 99%+ European and

40%+ British Isles. If the guys in the room were randomly picking out bingo balls, some Asian, African and Native American should have shown up in at least one of my brothers' samples.

I am at least 70% British and solidly 25% Eastern Europe based on genealogical research. AncestryDNA told me I was 39% Scandinavian, 17% Irish and 16% Eastern Europe....(not to mention being 7% Southern European and 9% Italy/Greece). How can an American, like Andy Lee, be more British than me?

LOL! It is kind of like Victoria, British Columbia in Canada is more British than Great Britain itself. (Yes, that is something they brag about there.)

I guess all of my British ancestors just didn't want to marry outside the clan! In fact, my Dutch ancestors are probably mostly British too!

The truth may lie in the history of Britain resembling a melting pot of the ethnicities you mentioned: Scandinavia, Irish, Eastern European, etc. Your results reflect this mixing of ethnicities. For me, it is possible my ancestors intermarried with the same ethnic gene pool.

Is it true that all siblings should have basically the same ethnic DNA, barring differences in eye and skin color? Or is DNA similar to a fingerprint with each sibling having the same fundamentals but also with variations?

DNA is not like a fingerprint. Identical twins have different fingerprints but the same DNA.

Ethnicity is not DNA. Since siblings share about 50% of their DNA, you would expect at least 50% of their ethnicity to be the same. However, the other 50% could be vastly different.

Let's use an extreme case. 7 of your 8 Great Grandparents are European, and 1 was a Cherokee princess. On paper via genealogical records, you and your siblings would each be 1/8 Cherokee. After DNA testing, your results report you have 18% (3/16) Cherokee, but your brother has only 6% (1/16). Did something go wrong?

No, the variance in percentages is not unusual and is entirely possible in genetics. While DNA on average is passed down 50% to each generation, on an individual basis, the percentages vary.

Even grandparents, who on average we share 25% of our DNA with, when measured has been shown to be 20-30% inheritance from each one, in complementary pairs. Meaning, if you received 20% of your genes from your grandmother, you would receive 30% from your grandfather.

Siblings have a unique set of DNA from their ancestors even though they share all of the same ancestors. Since ethnicity is based on an analysis of that DNA, each sibling will have a different ethnicity profile. That ethnic variance may not reflect the paper records you have.

How do we increase the size of the reference database? Would testing the military help? If the military personnel reported their claimed ancestry and physical traits and their DNA matched others in a reference population, would it grow?

Most reference populations have some necessary criteria:

1. All 4 of your grandparents need to be from the same country/region. Immigrant countries like the US, Canada, and Australia do not count.

2. You should not have close relatives in the reference database. So if your grandfather was already in the reference database, you, your siblings, and your cousins would not be eligible.

To increase the size of a reference database, more people need to take a DNA test. Since the majority of people tested thus far have been from the United States, to increase the reference population size significantly, more South Americans, Europeans, Africans, and Asians need to take the DNA tests.

Compulsory testing (i.e., through the military) would provide many samples, but if the testers do not know their heritage (point #1) or are related to others who have previously tested (point #2), then they will not contribute to an increased reference population. Additionally, compulsory testing is not ethical.

SPECIFIC ETHNICITIES

Can a DNA test identify the difference between Irish, Scottish, and Welsh?

Unless there are some "pure" Irish, Scottish, or Welsh people, then distinguishing between them will be difficult. All of these populations descend from the ancient Celts. Ethnicity estimates start with the assumption that before transoceanic travel there was limited intermixing. While this may be true over long periods of time, there have been numerous punctuated influxes of foreign invaders which intermixed or pushed out native populations in the British Isles.

My DNA test found only 3% Scandinavian, but I am a stereotypical Irish ginger. How can I not have more Scandinavian DNA when Eric the Red and Leif Ericson were supposed to have been mostly responsible for bringing that fair-ginger, light-eyed thing over to us in the British Isles?

Two possible reasons to consider:

1. The Scandinavian part that is left is the red-haired gene. Since red hair is a recessive trait controlled by a single gene (whereas hair color, in general, is influenced by more than a dozen different genes), the portion of Scandinavian you have may just happen to include the red hair gene on chromosome 16.

2. Red hair in the British Isles may not be from Eric the Red. While the common folklore suggests that Eric the Red (or other Vikings) brought red hair over, from the literature I have read, the evidence is not definitive. Red hair may have originated within Celtic populations, or it may be a common Celtic-Germanic trait that is even older.

The bottom line is you probably cannot use any single trait to identify what a significant amount of your ethnicity is.

I have tested with multiple companies, and my ethnicity results vary widely between them. Why is that?

There are three primary reasons for the differences:

1. About 50% of the SNPs overlap between the tests with all of the companies. So each company is testing a different set of SNPs. Think of this as the ingredients for a batch of cookies (flour, sugar, butter).

2. Each company has a different reference population database that they are using to define their specific ethnicity mixture. Think of this as the amounts of each ingredient needed (½ cup, 1 Tablespoon).

3. Each company has their own algorithm or formula to calculate ethnicity. Think of this as the instructions for making the cookies (oven temperature, how long).

Just like a recipe, if you change up the ingredients, the proportions, or the instructions, you bake cookies that are very similar or vastly different. Yet, you are still going to have a cookie and not a milkshake. Ethnicity results are kind of like that.

I am from Denmark, but my maternal grandmother is half German and half Polish. I had 42% Scandina-

vian, 14% Eastern Europe, and 9% Western Europe ethnicity results. What does it mean that the test showed I have 35% Great Britain when no one from my known ancestry is from Great Britain?

Great Britain DNA is a broad mixture of Briton DNA, Scandinavian DNA (from the Viking invasions), and Continental European DNA (from the Norman and Roman invasions). So even before the time of mass travel, Great Britain had significant mixing of DNA. In fact, most places around the world had significant admixtures. It is not surprising that Great Britain showed up in your DNA since your Scandinavian ancestral relatives probably played a role in one or more incursions into that country.

The point to take away is to accept ethnicity results with a grain of salt. There simply is not anything that is pure Great Britain, pure Scandinavian, or pure anything. Humans have been intermixing and migrating since we started venturing out of the grasslands of East Africa. That we can puzzle out some evidence of ethnicity is a novelty, but it should not define you.

From a DNA test, can I then conclude that I had British ancestors from about 100-500 years ago? Or, would I need to research my paper family tree to confirm that?

The science of ethnicity testing is not accurate enough to draw that conclusion, especially when we already know of several historical events that would have put "foreign" DNA into Great Britain. If you have done a Y-DNA test and the haplogroup is exclusive to

Great Britain, then you would have a case that you have some ancestors from there.

Further investigation into paper documents may give you an answer; however, recognize that many of the events (Viking raids, Norman invasion, Angles and Saxon invasions) that brought other DNA to Great Britain predate the timeframe that you will find reliable records.

How can DNA companies cluster India, Pakistan, and Bangladesh into the South Asian ethnic group? There are almost 2 billion people in that population. Shouldn't there be more ethnicities in this area?

Not really. The results, and by extension the ethnicity groupings, are a condition of not having enough data from a reference population to separate South Asians (India and Pakistan) into subgroups, which is different from Southeast Asians (Vietnam, Thailand, Cambodia) or East Asians (Chinese, Koreans, Japanese). Having large ethnicity sets is actually a condition of being conservative with your science. It would be sketchy to distinguish population groups with only a few dozen in the reference set.

Why are the French and Germans lumped into one category?

They are lumped into one category because the French and Germans are very similar on a DNA level. While we define the countries distinctly today, going back just a few hundred years you have lots of kingdoms and duchies and vassals that make up the area occupied by modern France and Germany. There was much inter-marriage within the nobility between all of these microstates. Research further back in time, and you have the Frankish people (where France acquired its name) which were also the ancestors of many of the Germanic tribes.

What would Adolf Hitler's ancestry be? I read somewhere that Hitler had Jewish Ancestry on his father's side of the family and that he hated his father and that is why he turned against the Jews.

From the literature I have read, it seems that most historians do not give credence to the Jewish link. Although, there was a rumor of it when Hitler was alive, and he took steps to publicize a genealogy showing that he was not Jewish. My guess, since he was from Austria, he would show up as mostly northwestern European (French/German) with maybe some Scandinavian or Eastern European thrown in as well.

Why did AncestryDNA report me as 91% African while MyHeritage DNA put me at 89%?

On a continental level, the results are most definitely correct. The reference populations for AncestryDNA and MyHeritage DNA pertaining to most of the countries or regions in Africa are not large enough to give more refined results. You are not reading conflicting reports.

I have reviewed Horn of Africa DNA results, and companies tend to indicate ethnicity as Middle Eastern and North African. Why is that?

From a geographic standpoint, the Horn of Africa is just a short boat ride to the Arabian Peninsula and is the most hospitable route to Northern Africa. I am not surprised in the least with the Middle Eastern and North African classification.

As a general rule, your DNA is going to be more closely related to people who live closer together geographically. That closeness is related to the navigable paths. While countries directly south of the Sahara desert may be closer in distance to many North African countries, the Horn of Africa area is much closer via navigable paths.

Genetic genealogy is terrific because it brings together our knowledge of populations, history, geography, and so much more.

What is the best test for Australian Aboriginal heritage?

I am not sure there is a good one yet. A reliable ethnicity test depends on the reference population. There isn't a significant reference population for many peoples of the world (including most Native Americans, Australian Aborigines). If all four of your grandparents were Australian Aborigines, then you would be an excellent candidate to add to the reference population.

Apparently, all the DNA tests lump Greek and Italian together, which is ridiculous seeing how different they are. Is there any test available today that could tell me how much Greek I am?

The people of the Greek archipelago and the Italian peninsula have intermixed for thousands of years. So the DNA is all jumbled up. I doubt you would be able to find any company that could identify with any degree of certainty between Greek and Italian. Culturally, the two modern-day countries may be different, but genetically, there must be enough similarities as to be lumped together.

I am struggling to find a DNA test that gives in-depth analysis of each region and the countries within that area. For example, 11% of my DNA is from the Iberian Peninsula, but I do not know whether that is Spanish or Portuguese ancestry. What should I do?

Unfortunately, what you want is not to be had. Because every region intermixed with their respective neighbors, there is a lot of DNA that is indistinguishable beyond a regional or even a continental level.

The key to more refined results is expanding the size and accuracy of the reference populations. Reference populations are primarily made up of those who have all four grandparents from the same area in non-immigrant countries. Most people know with a relatively high degree of certainty where all of their grandparents were born. Even with this, many geographic areas still only have reference populations in the hundreds due to co-mingling of ethnicities.

If a DNA tester knew that all 8 great-grandparents or all 16 great-great-grandparents were from the same area, the accuracy of the reference population increases dramatically. While accuracy increases, the size of the reference population would decrease as fewer people have a 'pure' ethnic genetic inheritance and fewer still know who all 16 great-great-grandparents are. As such, at a certain size (less than 100?) a more accurate reference population becomes fairly useless for matching ethnicity with any degree of certainty.

MyHeritage DNA reports that I am 11.6% Greek. Since this is in the double digits, do you think that I have ANY Greek DNA?

Without researching what the reference population they used is, I would suggest the Greek classification actually means Mediterranean (Turkey, Greek, Southern Italy). So with 11% you probably have a great grandparent who was from the Eastern Mediterranean or surrounding areas. You ancestor may indeed be Greek, but do not be surprised if they are from one of the other countries mentioned.

Which DNA testing company has the most information about South America?

From what I have read, 23andMe has the largest international database. However, you may also try one of the European Ancestry subsidiaries. Many people in South America have recent European ancestors.

What I want to know is what part of Africa (country or region) the majority of my ancestors lived. Which DNA system do you feel should give me the most accurate information?

Right now, no testing company will give you stupendous results, because the number of African samples is relatively small. However, don't let that discourage you. When more people with African ancestry test, then the results will improve. Encourage more people in your network who suspect they have African heritage to take DNA tests. You will benefit, and so will everyone else.

Do you know which test would reveal most accurately if I have Ashkenazi ancestry?

All of the DNA testing companies have an Ashkenazi reference population. Ashkenazi is one of the few reference populations about which we have reliable data. I have not read any reports that indicate which is the most accurate because you would need a rock solid paper trail to compare with to make that determination.

My grandfather was mixed Cherokee Indian. My two sisters both took the AncestryDNA test. It showed no Native American. Why?

First, neither AncestryDNA nor any other testing company has a reliable reference population for Cherokee (or any of the US-based Native American tribes for that matter) to use as a comparison. The Native American reference populations that do appear in the test results are actually from natives in Central and South America and the Inuit.

Second, Cherokee tribal membership can be traced back to the Dawes Rolls of 1905 (probably the generation before your grandparents). Anyone who is on the Dawes Rolls is considered part of one of the five civilized tribes (Cherokee being one of them), whether they were descended from Native Americans or not. Likewise, anyone not on the rolls was considered not to be tribal members whether they had Native American heritage or not. There are several known instances where African Americans and Europeans made it on the Dawes Rolls whether by design or by fraud. Some were adopted into the tribes earlier; some snuck on to receive the potential tribal benefits.

Third, the Cherokee (and the other civilized tribes) were the most integrated of the Native Americans with the European colonists. There was much intermixing, and it would not surprise me to find that much of the Native American DNA has been lost in the mix of European DNA.

Any and all of these reasons together make it difficult to distinguish Native American DNA when your heritage is primarily from North America.

How can Native American be a DNA ethnicity when they are from Asia?

While the Native Americans did migrate from Asia, their DNA has some unique markers that are not shared by their Asian relatives. On a broad scale, Asia and America DNA is lumped together. However, they have been separated for a long enough time that American DNA is distinguishable from Asian DNA (most of the time).

My great-grandmother was a Native American (Lumbee nation) on her paternal side, and my great-grandmother was Cherokee. Three genera-tions later it does not show up on my DNA test. My results are complete B.S.

Either the reference populations used for comparison cannot distinguish the tribes your heritage belonged to or maybe your ancestors were not genetic Native Ameri-cans. There are many uncertainties in ethnicity. That does not make DNA testing BS.

How far back would I find US Native American if I have less than 1%? 8-9 generations?

For 1% ethnicity results, you will find that ancestor between 5 to 50 generations back. DNA passes down through recombination in a random manner. Dividing the DNA in half for each generation is only a population average, not an individual expectation.

If your Native American DNA is from the Y chromo-some, then there are specific haplogroups only Native Americans have. Those haplogroups originated about 10-20 thousand years ago.

At that time, the markers in the Americas diverge from those similar in East Asians.

If your Native American DNA it is from your autosomal DNA, determining where it appears on your family tree is less likely without a paper trail of genealogy. Unfortunately, Cherokee was the first written North American language, and it did not appear until the 1800s.

Recognize that the vast majority of the "family history" information that the genealogy websites are giving you based on your DNA is very generic.

If you are white, you're European. You may have other things way back, but you're mostly European. If you are black, you're African. You may have different ethnicities way back, but you're primarily African. You can look in the mirror. You do not need to waste 100 bucks.

The mirror might be lying. As several cosmetic companies have shown, there is a vast variety of skin shades that overlap between different areas of the world. You could be dark and be Indian or Australian Aborigine. Central and South Americans' skin appears in every shade from white like Europeans to black like Africans.

Ethnicity results are not the only reason to take a DNA test, nor is it even the best reason. DNA is a record of your relationships with other family members. That record is worth $100, or less when on sale.

Many African Americans, like myself, would like to know which country or regions some of their ancestors originate. Will a DNA test help us on this quest?

For specific nations, your results might be disappointing as determining particular localities beyond the continental level is currently difficult to impossible. However, when more people test who are descendants of native African populations, then the reference populations of the DNA testing companions can grow and increase the accuracy of ethnicity estimates. Eventually, you could have results that determine a specific region in Africa that your ancestors lived.

If you know any first generation African immigrants, then encourage them to test. If you travel to African countries, invite the people you associate with to test. Become an advocate that creates the change you want to have happen for all individuals with ties to Africa.

Why does it appear that DNA companies focus more on white Europeans and do not collect much data on people from Asia, Middle East, or African countries?

DNA companies collect data on whomever tests. They cannot improve their databases until more Asian, Middle Eastern, and African countries test. Additionally, most of the testing companies originated in countries with significant populations of European origins. As each company expands globally, the impression of favoring specific ethnic groups will decrease.

It is also possible that countries with predominantly white European have more lenient laws regarding DNA testing than countries with the ethnicities you listed. A company may want to expand into Asia, the Middle

East, and Africa but sovereign nations may prevent them.

UNASSIGNED ETHNICITIES

Family Tree DNA reports that I am 99% European and 1% of a trace region. Just curious, what is that?

That extra 1% means a testing company could not determine within their certainty threshold of where the DNA originated. In other words, several disparate groups probably share that same segment or a very similar segment of DNA. Statistically, these percentages are low, and thus the likelihood of the ethnicity being background noise in the algorithm is high. I would not claim 1% is an accurate representation of my ancestry.

My MyHeritage DNA results include 14 percent 'other,' What does that mean? Am I from another planet?

Sorry, you are not an alien. 'Other' usually means you have somewhat generic DNA and thus no group can claim it. As more people take DNA tests and reference populations increase, you should notice the 'other' amount decrease.

Do you think that with time they will assign that unassigned % to something?

Yes. Once they have a reference population that it matches, the unallocated percentage will be classified. However, this eventuality may take few years.

USES OF ETHNICITY RESULTS

My ethnicity results are nearly identical at Ancestry DNA, Family Tree DNA, My Heritage DNA, and Living DNA. They all show me much more Irish than I ever thought I was. After doing more genealogical research, I found Irish ancestors in all 8 of my great-grandparents' heritage.

Awesome. Your research shows one of the positive things that the ethnicity results can reveal. If there is a significant amount (>5-10%) of something that you did not already know about, you have an excellent clue to research ancestors from that location.

I am from the Middle East, but I know from our family history that I have: Egyptian, Turkish, Indonesian, Indian, Israeli/Palestinian blood. I am curious whether or not I have any southern European origins. Which company should I use?

Any of them will work. The problem you will run into is whether the reference populations for each company can distinguish between Egyptian, Turkish, Israeli/Palestinian, and Southern European (likely Greece and Italy). Since they all surround the Mediterranean Sea and ocean travel was the fastest form of long-distance travel up until the last two centuries, the mixture of these populations has been happening for millennia. In other words, what a DNA company labels as southern European, might just be Turkish or Middle Eastern.

Will testing companies provide a tree of people I am related to?

No DNA test will ever tell you your family history. You are going to have to spend some time digging through documents and talking with relatives to find that out.

My mother has a German maiden surname, but her DNA tests report no German ethnic percentages. Some companies indicated Ashkenazi Jew. A DNA health report revealed a rare genetic disease that is common among people with Middle Eastern and Jewish backgrounds. What would you conclude from these ethnic puzzle pieces?

Without examining your results, I could only speculate on why no German is showing up.

First, Germany did not exist as we know it today until 1871. Additionally, numerous Germanic tribes mixed with a variety of ethnic groups, complicating the reference populations.

Next, France/Germany is the major group of Northwest Europe as reported on 23andMe. If you have Northwestern Europe results, that may reveal your missing German DNA.

Next, Germany was also part of Prussia and Austria and stretched across Poland and into Russia at one point in time. If you had Eastern European DNA results, this might indicate your ethnic identity and also suggest your family adopted a German surname at the time.

Another possibility is a population moved into Germany in the past, adopted the language, but primarily married within their group (something like the Roma, or a religious group), so they do not show up as German.

The history of Germany reveals the complications of defining it as an ethnic group before 1871. Your missing German heritage is an excellent example of why you can not use DNA by itself to solve genealogical problems, DNA has to be used in conjunction with other records.

Regarding the Jewish clues, consider another population. Sephardic Jew is another population that probably doesn't register like Ashkenazi, and many databases do not have a reference population for it.

Why waste your money on a DNA test if the ethnicity results are not clear or provide country-level results?

If all you want is your ethnicity, you should not spend the money. DNA testing is much more valuable for finding matches with distant cousins that you would not find otherwise.

What about for African Americans who descend from slaves? There are no records past a certain point in time to do any genealogical research. How do DNA tests help us?

DNA helps us understand a little of our history before the recorded history begins. Europeans may have records that extend back hundreds of years, but at some point, they also stop. Native Americans, Polynesians, and other global tribal cultures did not have any written language until the 1800s. Some aboriginal peoples still do not use written languages. Some ethnic groups had their records destroyed during political upheavals throughout the history of the world. In short, descendants of American slaves are not the only groups with paper brick walls.

DNA helps everyone connect to the past. DNA may not tell us specific people or places, but it joins us to the broader human family through time.

Definitions

The study of any subject will involve a terminology that needs to be understood. Below is the most common jargon used throughout the book. Some terms could include a much more extensive explanation, but I have tried to simplify them as much as possible.

Admixture or **Ethnicity** or **Heritage**: The mixing of different population groups that detected when comparing DNA to reference populations. These results are usually reported as a percentage. The terms are interchangeable.

Allele: One of two versions of the same gene that express a different trait (i.e., blood type A vs. O).

Autosomal DNA or **atDNA**: Chromosomes 1 through 22 which are passed from parents to children after undergoing a process of recombination. The most common DNA tests are Autosomal DNA tests. This type of DNA is beneficial when matching relatives to 5th or 6th cousins.

Background noise: DNA that can not be easily classified as a specific ethnicity. The unclassified DNA is a result of humans sharing a significant portion of DNA and population groups having been intermixed extensively for hundreds and thousands of years.

Base Pair: The chemical that joins two strands of DNA (i.e., the rungs of the ladder). Adenine, Cytosine, Guanine, and Thymine, usually abbreviated as A, C, T, G. A joins with T and C joins with G.

Centimorgan (cM): A measure of genetic distance that is related to how likely a recombination event will occur.

Chromosome: A structure of DNA that contains a number of genes. Humans have 23 pairs of chromosomes (for a total of 46 chromosomes).

Close relationship: For genealogical purposes, 2nd cousins or closer. Based on statistical analysis and DNA test data, each person shares some amount of DNA with all of their close relationships.

DNA: Deoxyribonucleic Acid, a chemical found in living organisms that codes for all of the traits and processes of life. DNA is in the shape of a double helix, which resembles a twisted ladder.

Double cousin: 1st cousins that share both sets of grandparents but different parents (for instance brothers who married sisters). Double cousins share twice the amount of DNA as full cousins. Double cousins can also be 2nd or more cousins.

Full-match: Segments of DNA where a large number of SNPs match both letters between two people. Full-match segments only occur in siblings and double cousin relationships.

Genealogy: The study of family relationships.

Gene: A segment of DNA that codes for a protein (i.e., a trait like blood type or hair color). Humans have approximately 25,000 genes which make up about 3% of the genome.

Genome: The complete set of DNA in an organism. In humans, this would include all 23 pairs and the mitochondrial DNA.

Half-match: Segments of DNA where a large number of SNPs match one of two letters between two people.

Half-relationship: Half-siblings share a single parent. Half the amount of expected shared DNA as a full-relationship. Half relationships occur throughout the family tree (i.e., half-uncles, half-cousin, half-niece).

Haplogroup: A group of people who share a common patrilineal or matrilineal ancestor based on DNA that is passed down without recombination (i.e., Y-DNA, mtDNA). Haplogroups are used to study the migration of the human population over time.

Matrilineal: The female line of ancestors through the mother. The matrilineal line is identified through mitochondrial DNA.

Megabases (Mb): Millions of base pairs (not the same measurement as cM), used to order chromosomes, an absolute measurement of position.

Microarray chip: The tool used to read the SNPs of a DNA sample. Depending on how they are configured, chips may have several hundred thousand SNPs.

Mitochondrial DNA or **mtDNA**: A circular DNA structure (different from chromosomes) located in the mitochondria of the cell. Mitochondrial DNA is passed from mother to children.

No-match: Segments of DNA where a significant number of SNPs do not match either of two letters between two people.

Patrilineal: The male line of ancestors through the father. The patrilineal line is identified through Y-DNA.

Phasing: A process to determine which sequences of DNA are attributable to each parent. Useful for dividing the pair of chromosomes into separate paternal and maternal chromosomes so that matches can be assigned to one of the parents.

Recombination: During cell division, a process by which portions of paired chromosomes swap places so that the daughter chromosome is a combination of both the mother and father chromosome. Also called crossover.

Reference population: A set of people who identified as originating from a specific area. To determine admixture results, a DNA test is compared to various reference populations to decide which ones it most closely matches.

SNP: Single Nucleotide Polymorphism, a point (base pair) on the genome where differences have occurred (i.e., an A instead of a C, or a deletion instead of a letter). Usually reported as two letters, one from each paired chromosome. Pronounced "snip."

STR: Short Tandem Repeats, a string of repeating letters that vary in the number of repetitions. Changes infrequently from one generation to the next. Similar lengths across several markers indicate the degree of separation. Found in non-coding regions. Pronounced "stir."

Triangulation: A genetic genealogy comparison process where three people match each other at the same location. The matching segments indicate that all three inherited that portion of DNA from a common ancestor.

X-DNA: One of the two sex chromosomes. Females have two X chromosomes, one identical to their father's and one from their mother passed on through recombination. Males receive one recombined X chromosome from their mother.

Y-DNA: One of the two sex chromosomes. Males receive a Y chromosome identical to their father.

About the Authors

Devon Noel Lee specializes in preserving and sharing family memories and motivating budding genealogists. She has created and published 60 scrapbooks, written a memoir from her teenage years and four family history how-to books, including the popular *A Recipe for Writing Family History*. She has written the stories for over 120 ancestors and counting and is working on compiling many of them into a book. Devon is a high energy speaker and lab instructor at local, state, national genealogy conferences and public libraries. She educates and inspires the genealogy world through videos at FamilyHistoryFanatics.com. She graduated from Texas A&M with degrees in Marketing and Journalism. Currently, Devon is a home educator for five superheroes.

Andy Lee has been involved in family history for 30 years and wrote a contest winning essay about an American Revolution ancestor while in high school. As a member of Toastmaster's International, Andy has achieved the status of Competent Communicator and won several storytelling contests. He has given presentations throughout the US and Canada to professional organizations, university classes, local genealogy societies, family history conferences, and Boy Scout organizations. He's the co-author of *A Recipe for Writing Family History* and contributes to the FamilyHistoryFanatics.com YouTube channel. Andy graduated from Texas A&M University with a degree in Mechanical Engineering.

Made in the USA
San Bernardino, CA
12 February 2018